This book is dedicated to Folashade Omolayo Olawumi, Kehinde Orishayomi, Anais Durand, and everyone who has helped me, in any shape or form along the way.

RENT2RENT
MASSIVE CA$H DURING A MASSIVE CRASH

*How to make £10K a month
without the sweat*

TAIWO ORISHAYOMI

authorHOUSE®

AuthorHouse™
1663 Liberty Drive
Bloomington, IN 47403
www.authorhouse.com
Phone: 1-800-839-8640

Published by AuthorHouse   04/19/2012

ISBN: 978-1-4678-8933-9 (sc)
ISBN: 978-1-4678-9005-2 (e)

Employ your time in improving yourself by other men's writings so that you shall come easily by what others have laboured hard for.

(Socrates)

Rent2Rent is my account of how I created a stream of passive income for myself in property during the economic market crash. Within a year, my cash cow grew from £0 a month to £10,000 a month. This is my story; this is my journey.

My house references which will be referred to throughout this book are:

KIM40

NEW61

LOD47

BRE37

DOW14

BOS1

BOS9

BOS71

BOS78

DOU54

GLOS579

FIL949

SPR28

CHU78

When I decided to write this book, I was still searching for the dreams I had held in my mind for as long as I could remember. I had had two recurring dreams for the past twenty years—one I entitled *The Chase*. In this dream, I found myself running for dear life. Even though I had the power to cruise above houses, I was still running. I always woke up distressed whenever I had this dream. My second recurring dream was what I called *Money in my Garden*. That was literally what that dream was about. I would wake up in my dream with a cup of coffee in my hand. I would plan my day and I would stroll into my garden. I would unearth a bit of grass and under the roots were lots of golden coins. I would ask myself if I should unearth one more just in case I spent more money that day. There were variations to this dream though. Sometimes I would be walking along a stream and would find lots of golden coins. Other times, I would compete with friends about who could find the most coins in a stream. I always won. A few times the variation had been simply plucking money from a tree in my garden. Instead of leaves, there were thousands of banknotes.

Some people always have the feeling of being poor, but I have always had the feeling of being rich, even when I have had no money in my pocket. Since I was a child, I knew that money would surely come to me easily; I have always seemed to be able to attract that. I have worked since I was thirteen years old, cleaning other people's houses and babysitting. When I was at the university, I was already supporting my lifestyle; I was able to save 60 per cent of my earnings, and by the time I finished my studies, four years later, I had saved £5,000 and was not in debt like many of my friends. It is easy to make money; also, it is easy not to have any.

When I decided to quit my job in February 2010, I knew I wanted to focus on making an endless passive income, which would enable me to focus on my family when I decided to start one. Property was my only answer at that time. Twelve months later, I had succeeded in achieving my goal of MPI. I moved from a salary of £30,000 per annum working from 8 a.m. to 5 p.m., five days a week, to £120,000 per annum in passive income, working sporadically and being in charge of my own time.

Those who have attended some of my training days already know some of the techniques I am about to reveal in this book. Other techniques have never being revealed. My goal is to demonstrate that passive income is not a utopia; it is achievable rather easily, but one must be in the right industry and willing to learn with the right people. I will guide you through my ups and downs during those twelve months. You will read about my desperate attempts to crack the property industry. Whilst deeply frustrated, I now know that those feelings of despair were indications that I was stretching out of my comfort zone. So whenever you feel down, understand that that is a normal feeling successful people have at some point on their journey. That is you, pulling out of the mass market and making your way towards the avenue of success.

This is my story over the period of a year. This is how I became financially stable. This is how I created my cash cow, which has now enabled me to move to the next step of my dream.

I hope this book will inspire you to follow your bliss. You must ask yourself these questions over and over again: What am I good at? How can I make passive income out of it?

Write these questions down and stick them on your fridge, put them in your handbag or wallet, stick them by your bed so that you can see them and feel them over and over again. In these hard economic times, you must not think of what to do if you lose your job but rather, if you are business-minded, think of how to become self-employable, because there is no job security anywhere. If you are self-employed, no boss can fire you; you are your own boss. You are independent and free from continuous fear. Your only risk is entrusting your financial stability to someone else, i.e., your boss.

Once you have nailed down the correct answer for you, find a way to start a business out of it. You may struggle for a few months, probably the first year, but *do not give up* because every day is pushing you towards success. Any failure you experience is part of the process. There is no success without failure.

Find that passion, and find a way to make money out of it. My passion is management. I love to manage people, and above all, I love to manage problems.

Your mindset

In order to create Massive Passive Income (MPI) you must have a mindset that prepares you for the ride. *Despite my massive success in creating my MPI,* some people in the property industry do not believe that my strategy can work the way I present it. Some of these people have already have several HMOs (houses of multiple occupancy), and they cannot grasp why other property owners would submit their houses to me. There are others who would argue for hours to prove to me that this strategy cannot be done in their area.

If you have read Richard Branson's autobiography, "losing My Virginity", you will notice some characteristics that have made him the multimillionaire that he is today. The man just cannot and will not take no for answer. Rejection is never an obstacle.

Your mindset determines your level of success in life. Once I understood that, my life changed completely.

This is my journey. This is how I made over £10,000 a month in passive income within a year during the biggest economic crash, some people say, in history. I am now coaching others to do the same. I hope to meet you one day and to have the honour of coaching you too.

Chapter I

BABY STEPS

Rich Dad Poor Dad by Robert T. Kiyosaki:

A Life-Changing Book

January-September 2010

I came across this book through an online personal development course I was doing at the time. The book was always quoted by wealth speakers. I decided to purchase it from a second hand bookstore near where I lived.

As soon as I started reading it, I knew it would change my life totally. I had read and listened to Napoleon Hill on YouTube, I had read and reread *Think and Grow Rich*, I had read *As Man Thinketh*, *The Richest Man in Babylon*, and dozens of other wealth books, but none moved me as much as *Rich Dad Poor Dad* did. That book had changed the life of everyone that I knew had read it. I also read volume 5 of the Rich Dad series, *Rich Dad's Retire Young Retire Rich* by the same author

As if it were meant to be, after reading the books, I received an email from Marcus de Maria, one of the wealth coach trainers to whom I usually listen. He sent an email inviting people to listen to a property webinar. I tuned in on D-day and discovered the Duo: two young guys who seemed to be as hungry as I was. One of them spoke that night and I was hooked for good on the idea of using a property portfolio to reach millions of people. This was in January 2010.

My First Seminar with the Duo: I Bought Their Two Books (February 2010)

The webinar was encouraging and quite an eye opener. I decided to attend the seminar the Duo was offering. Their offer was to buy a ticket for £47 for two people. The seminar was to take place in Oxford Street, London, a few weeks later. I was not sure who to invite as a guest, so I asked myself who I would want to enlighten the most. My twin sister was an option but she already knew everything I knew. We were part of the same online personal development group. The other option was to invite a friend. I chose to invite a friend instead.

On the specified day in February, we arrived at the seminar half an hour early and took the time just to relax in front of a coffee. I was excited because I was going to learn about properties.

The seminar was to last the whole day, from 9.30 a.m. until 5.00 p.m. The place was jam-packed with minds as equally hungry as mine. I sat through the first two hours feeling like an ogre looking for food; in my case, I was looking for knowledge. My guest was dozing off; I couldn't believe it! she decided to leave after the first break at 12 p.m. My opinion was that anyone who did not want to be here should leave and make way for those who really value this free education. I later asked her why she did not find the program interesting. She answered that she did not believe that such young men had bought over 200 properties. I said that that sort of thinking was exactly what makes the large majority of the population poor. Most people want to see before they believe, while the successful few believe then they see it. This is the difference between the rich and the poor. When we believe something, that is when our reality and the universe reshape themselves to allow a way for those beliefs to become reality. A person who waits to believe will wait a lifetime. This reminds me of a book I read quite a while ago called *Conversations with God*, by Donald Walsh. In it he says we are God. Human beings have the power to create whatever we wish to create, but 99.9 per cent of the world's population would rather pray to a God they have never seen. Even the Bible says that God has created us in his own image. What this means is that whatever God can do, we can do it too.

Coming back to the situation with my friend, I decided to leave it as it was; only time will tell if she ever changes her mind.

I Read Both Books: Confusion and Hunger

After the Duo's seminar, I decided to purchase their books. I read both of them with equal enthusiasm; I decided to seek further knowledge by booking into a three-day workshop with them in Peterborough. I was hungry! I felt that I had wasted too much time doing other things so far. I felt I had to run twice as fast because the Duo was the same age as I, and I felt far behind. I had to catch up as fast as I could.

Master Class: Three-day Intensive Training;
Sometime in May 2010

By the time I went to the master class, I had left my day job, which had been an agonising experience for me for a whole year. I was working as a sales manager and a marketing manager for a publication in Bristol. I did not respect the owner because he lacked business sense and the team I was working with was short of knowledge when it came to business. I could no longer bear the gossip, the minimal effort and above all, I could no longer bear my alarm clock ringing at 6.30 a.m.

I wanted to wake up when I wanted to, go to work when I wanted, work from home if I wanted, and above all, I wanted to be my own boss again.

While booking the master class course, I did not have enough in my bank account to pay the £1770 required. This was in March. At the same time, I received the news that my biological father had died of a heart attack in Nigeria. I was his first child; my twin sister was pregnant so I had to make the trip back home. This was quite a costly and unexpected event; I had to find over £1500 to pay for all the expenses and at the same time lose three weeks of freelance work I had lined up. I explained the situation to the Duo and they accepted a deposit of £500 and a £100 monthly payment for a year.

I was glad we could reach a mutual arrangement.

D-day arrived; I had booked into a b. & b. in Peterborough and had driven there, that being the easiest option. The first day was the longest. We crammed so much information in our brains that I could literally hear my brain asking me for a break. The refreshment was delicious and on time.

The second day was equally charged; having made a few contacts and friends, interaction was a lot easier. The whole group was great.

The third day was a one-to-one session where we were all given the core ingredient software. This allowed us to locate our goldmine areas, analyse deals, and make good judgment on any deal before buying. We were also given a file, which contained the whole three-day education and much more. That became a tool for a short while in my journey.

Bridging Loan Finance: Study

I met Rory O'Mara during my first seminar with the Duo. Rory owns a bridging loan company called Closed Bridging Finance. At first, I did not understand what this company does. I requested further explanation from Rory, and he sent me a handout explaining exactly what it does and how property investors could incorporate it into their systems. After receiving this PDF file, I became so acquainted with the system that I was able to attempt to use it on one of my prospective buys.

I Built My First Website: My Webmaster Disaster

My first property website was a template I bought online. A friend of mine, Nico, convinced me to go for this particular template. He told me how easy it would be to control through Joomla CMS. Being a friend, I trusted him with the job. I gave £200 for the project. I knew the template would cost a maximum of £50; the rest was for his couple of hours' time to set it up.

I got another friend of mine to create my logo and design my business card and leaflets. I directed her to create the look I wanted for my business. My motto was, fake it till I make it. I needed to look successful at the networking events I was going to be attending. I searched Google's small business networking in my area. Quite a few businesses came up, so I contacted them asking to attend their next events. The networking events were very good at pushing me out of my lonely but ambitious world and allowing me to compare myself to other like-minded people. I quickly understood that that was not the way forward for me in particular. I needed to meet struggling landlords whom I could help. They were not at business networking events. So I decided to distribute leaflets in my Goldmine areas instead. I printed 5,000 colourful leaflets using the design my friend had created for me a few weeks earlier, put on my walking shoes, and started walking around my chosen area. Very quickly, barking dogs became a familiar tune; my main concern was to avoid having my fingers bitten off by an angry dog. I distributed my first batch of 5,000, and then I decided that my time was more valuable, so I outsourced that part to David. I had met David leafleting in my chosen area, so I approached him to find out if he could add my leaflets to his pile. His answer was yes. We agreed on a comfortable price and that is how David became part of my team.

Now that I had more time, I decided to work on the estate agents, as I was taught by my gurus. I would contact them one by one, book a viewing, dress smartly for the viewings, and chat with them. Remember, these were my early days and I thought that I had sufficient knowledge to buy a property. Little did I know, I was miles away from achieving that goal. The dish of the day at that time was NMD, meaning *no money down*. I thought I could buy without putting any of my own money into the deal, as I was taught was possible. So all my energy went to finding a BMV, meaning a *below market value* property. If I could find a property that was 30 per cent BMV, then I could get a mortgage at the full price. The extra 30 per cent would cover all my legal and I could have some cash back in my pocket too. Naively, I believed the whole story and later on discovered that this practice was Illegal too. So I changed my tune there and then.

Being Part of the Crew: Gaining Knowledge

June-September 2010

During this period, I knew that I did not know much about what I was doing, so I decided to crew for free for a while with the Duo. I went to most of their events to help out. I was not paid; it even cost me money to help them. I had to pay my transport to get to the event, pay for my meals and accommodation, but I knew that I was in the right environment to keep the burning fire alive. The more I crewed, the more familiar faces I met, and the more I was considered an investor. My confidence started growing because people who were where I had been just a few months before started asking me questions which, to my surprise, I could answer satisfactorily. So I started to build a list of contacts of people who usually call me to ask for advice. Bear in mind that at this stage I was faking it! People thought that I had bought many properties. I was just glad to be one step above those arriving after me. And I was glad to help too.

Being Part of the Crew: Gaining Confidence

October 2010

My confidence grew more and more as I crewed. I was mingling with people who had thirty, fifty, one hundred property portfolios. I had a list of mortgage advisers of whom I could ask questions.

During this period, I was viewing many properties with estate agents, putting in offers at least 30 per cent below market value just to see if anyone was desperate enough to sell. The more properties I viewed, the more my confidence grew. Then I understood that in any business, confidence could take you far even if you do not know much.

Lead Generation Website: Being in Control

Between all my crewing and viewings, I came across an email sent by Rory regarding a lead generation website. This was to drive traffic to my website. I thought that was a way of leveraging my time. I could visit the estate agents but also allow private sellers to find me via my website. So I bought the training for £200 and started promoting my website. I had to learn the technical side of SEO. I did this for some weeks then decided I was better off just outsourcing this part too. Those were £200 wasted. The lesson I learned was to stick to what I was naturally good at doing.

Google Adwords: Thanks HSBC

During this time, I received a letter from my bank offering a £75 voucher to start a Google Adword campaign. I took the offer and opened an account. Funny enough, many people found me through this. So I decided to invest £5 per day in that. Below are some of the private sellers who found me through this system. I am not promoting Google by the way.

Two Six-bedroom Houses in Bristol: The E's Story

Mr E and son came across my ad via Google ads. I was very surprised to see my Google ads work so quickly. Mr E and son wanted to sell two big six-bedroom houses located in Stoke Gifford, north of Bristol. I booked to view the properties the following day. I arrived fifteen minutes in advance as usual. The two houses were rebuilt entirely by Mr E and son who are both builders. When I went in, I thought this must be a good lead to sell to any HMO investor. Mr E explained to me how much they were getting in revenue on a monthly basis and yearly basis. The two properties yield almost £5,000 a month in profit. The expenses are around £1470 per month. The two houses are fully tenanted, which is a good selling point.

I sent this to an investor friend of mine:

Stoke Gifford

Filton, Bristol

BS34

Deal type: HMO

A six-bedroom property with a possibility to make it seven-bedroom with loft conversion. Completely and newly refurbished to the highest standard. Glass conservatory overlooking a large garden. Fully tenanted with professionals. Requires no work whatsoever except for the loft conversion if you wish to add another room. Fully furnished.

Two double rooms with ensuite bathrooms

Three large double rooms

One large single room

Gas central heating

Wireless Internet throughout

Double-glazing

Lounge

Kitchen dinner

Downstairs cloakroom

Upstairs bathroom with bath and WC

Private front house garage with space for four cars or six smaller ones

Financials:

Market value: £325,000

Purchase price: £290,000

Instant equity: £35,000

Current monthly rental: £2,417

Current monthly expenses: £375

Reservation fee: £995

Finder's fee: £3,995

Other costs: Usual purchase costs including solicitors, brokers etc. (approx. £3,000 for a no-money-down deal)

Contact: Taiwo Orishayomi on 07727 671 000

After speaking with my friend Jay, he pointed out a few issues that made it unsellable. He said that to sell the deal, the reduction had to be at least 30 per cent BMV, bringing the selling price down to £210K.

I knew at this point that the only thing I could do was to buy the properties for myself and rent them out as HMOs hence taking me out of my strategy.

Mr E and son are very proud of and emotionally attached to both properties, having built them. They hoped to sell them for the 2008 valuation, which was just impossible in the 2010 market. They were looking for £600K on properties worth £450-£500K. When I told them this, they seemed to be very shocked and insulted. I felt like I had just told them their children were ugly!

I realised that many vendors today are totally out of touch with the reality. Most of them still believe that they are sitting on a positive equity.

Coming back to Mr E and son, they were looking for an investor who would just give them £600K for both properties. Here is the math:

Current yearly yield on both properties is £49,008. Mr E and son think this is good return for any investor.

Here is what an investor sees: I leave £600K in two properties and earn £49,008 a year. Or I invest £600K in 120 properties (minimum with that sort of capital). If each property yields the minimum of £2,000 a year, 120 would yield £240K a year plus the increase in value of 120, which could potentially double in the long run.

The moral of the story is that an investor with £600K would be foolish to invest all that money in just two properties.

My last meeting with Mr E and son was in my office where I suggested an arrangement that would allow me to buy the properties from them, give them a lump sum of money, as they needed to start the extension of their own house, and give them tax release over the next two years. This was the proposal:

Assisted deposit/part refund buying processes explained:

I)   Parties involved: Assisted deposit

      A mortgage company to provide 75 per cent of the money

      Assisted deposit company: to provide 25 per cent of the money

      Vendor's solicitor (paid by us)

      Investor's solicitor

      Surveyor

II) Parties involved: Part refund process

Vendor

Investor

Solicitor

The process of part I:

The assisted deposit company will send out an independent surveyor who will value the property. Once the report of the surveyor is received by the assisted deposit company, the sale is negotiated down to 30 per cent below the current market value. The sale has to go through at a minimum of 30 per cent as a rule. This is because of the falling of the property market.

For example, if the surveyor says the property is worth £300,000, the assisted deposit company will only get involved if the vendor accepts to sell at £210,000.

The mortgage lender will not be informed of the selling price but of the surveyor price. The sale of the property will be officially £300,000. This prevents any devaluation of properties in the area.

This strategy allows the investor to get more money out of the banks and allows a fast sale.

The process of part II:

This is a unique agreement between the vendor and the investor only.

The investor agrees to give one-third of the 30 per cent below market value back within 2-3 years. This agreement is signed in front of a solicitor.

For example: £300,000-£210,000 = £90,000 (30%)

£90,000 / 3 = £30,000

Within 2-3 years, £30K will be returned to the vendor. This sale is guaranteed whether the property market crashes or not. The remaining money is secured against the property.

Conclusion:

In reality, the vendor only drops 20 per cent and not 30 per cent. This allows the vendor to move forward and the investor to buy without locking in a great deal of deposit.

The property is sold for £240,000 guaranteed no matter the economic condition.

The benefits for you includes less Capital Gain Tax to pay when you exchange.

Mr E and son said no. I wished them the very best of luck, knowing that they were not motivated enough to sell.

One Three-bedroom in Bath: The K's Story

The Ks also found me via my Google ads. My Google ads were doing very well and I was paying just £5 a day. Anyway, the K family called me; actually it was Mrs K who called. Mrs K was a student nurse and Mr K a builder who had been severely hit by the economy, due to the lack of new constructions. The K family lived on less than £17K a year salary.

When I did my research, I found that they had bought the property in 1999 for £52K. They have now run a debt of over £197K on it. They kept withdrawing money out of the property to cater for the extensions or perhaps for the holidays. Today, their property is worth less than what they owe on it. If the interest rate goes up, they will be out of their home.

The Ks can't afford to sell for less than the amount they owe, which makes it very hard to find a solution. I have explained this to them and they have been thinking of getting on the council list. I will keep in touch with them from time to time to see how they are doing.

Leafleting Expert?

My first batch of leaflets was done the expensive way. I wanted it to be well done, glossy, and colourful. A batch of 5,000 cost me almost £200. I thought that was a fair price until I saw a far better price on SingingPig, a popular forum for property investors in the UK. Paul Clark Printing Ltd was recommended on the forum. I got 50,000 black and white leaflets printed for £163, which was enough stock to last me eight months at least.

My second attempt at distributing my leaflets, the costly 5,000, was done through an agent I found on the street. I approached someone distributing leaflets and asked him if he would like to work for me; he then handed me the leaflet he was distributing which contained the agent's name. I called them, spoke to Chris, and arranged an appointment at my office for the following week.

I was considering using them on a regular basis, until Chris showed up. He made no effort whatsoever to dress up properly; he looked like a builder on a hot summer day. I decided not to judge and gave him the benefit of the doubt. I paid him £150 plus VAT and received not one single call from his work.

I asked Chris to email me the list of streets where my leaflets were distributed; he sent me a map with some highlighted spots on it weeks after my request. I decided not to bother with them any longer. Chris did not even attempt to call me again for more business.

While I was viewing another property, I found David, a short Afghan man, distributing leaflets. I asked him if he would like to work for me, to which he said yes. I negotiated the going rate there and then, £30 for 1,000 leaflets.

I told him that I would be printing some leaflets soon and would call him once they were ready.

Three weeks later David called and asked me if the leaflets had arrived. I said no, but I would keep him updated. Three weeks after that, David called me again and I told him the same thing. Two weeks later, my leaflets from Paul Clark arrived, I called David in, and he started straight away. Within the first day, I received a call from someone who had noticed my leaflets dumped in a building. I asked him for more details about the building, to which he told me that only refugees and homeless people lived there, none of whom had any property to sell. After that, I called David in and explained what I expected from him. I asked him to focus only on houses, not buildings. He was okay with that.

The third time David came to my office, he was more lively and touchy than the previous times. He then asked me if I was married. I said no but that I was engaged. David's English was very bad, which made his rude request pardonable. He asked me if I wanted to be his girlfriend, I pretended not to understand and then told him that I had no girlfriend looking for a boyfriend. The next time I met him, I kept a long distance and he never attempted to come on to me again.

The other calls I got from David's work were quite satisfactory. I received a call from Mr and Mrs W, who wanted to sell their bungalow in order to move closer to their daughter, and another call from Mr and Mrs E, who also wanted to sell their house because they wanted to move into a bungalow near the sea. Mr E had knee problems, which did not allow him to go up and down the stairs.

Mr and Mrs W's Three-bedroom Bungalow

Mr and Mrs W called me through my leafleting. They had had their property on the market for over six weeks with a local estate agency. Their three-bedroom bungalow was initially listed for £137,000, which they brought down after four weeks to £127K.

Mr and Mrs W were an elderly couple who married over thirty-two years ago. Mrs W had had a stroke recently, which was what prompted them to move closer to their daughter in Whitchurch. They explained that they had found another bungalow near their daughter and would like to buy it. I asked them if they had any mortgage on their bungalow, to which they answered no. They had bought it seven years before, in 2004, for £115K and they wished to sell it for at least £125K.

There was a possibility of transforming the bungalow into a 2-storey house later on.

When I met the couple, Mrs W was extremely nice, but Mr W was a bit reserved. I explained to them the state of the market. As they were an elderly couple, I was very honest and told them that if they did not need to sell, then they should hold on for a few more years. I told them that I would go and work the figures and then call them back the following day. I think they appreciated my non-pushy style.

The following day, I went to see them with an offer of 30 per cent BMV, bringing the sale price to £89,250. They immediately said no. I was glad they rejected my offer because I was reluctant to see such an elderly couple getting into the mortgage market. They were happy with my advice. I said they should reconsider selling in about five years' time but certainly not in today's market.

I told them that if they knew of anyone willing to sell quickly, they should let me know. We parted feeling very happy. I was contented because this old couple will remain in the security of their home, and I think they were quite relieved at the idea of not having to move out.

Mr and Mrs E's two-bedroom Boutique House

Mr and Mrs E also called me through my leaflet. Mr E contacted me and explained the perfect condition of their property. I booked in a viewing for the following day, in the evening.

I arrived at Gadshill Road fifteen minutes early. The house was beautifully presented with a very clean front patio. Mr E opened the door for me; immediately the welcoming perfume made me want to live in the property. The decor was sumptuous, making the little house look like a boutique Parisian cottage. The wallpaper was from Designer Guild, I could tell, and there was a different wallpaper colour for every single room. Mr E showed me the front room, the lounge leading to the kitchen, and the garden. The kitchen floor was in porcelain tiles, the appliances in stainless steel, the lounge and front room floor in treated wood which I had never seen before. He told me that the floor had a lifetime guarantee I just had to take off my shoes.

He then led me upstairs to two beautiful double rooms where I met Mrs E, a well preserved, elegant woman.

We all went downstairs to discuss business. The Es are in their 50s. They bought the house for £100K in 2004. Their house had been with Haart Fishponds for six weeks and had not sold. They said they would be terminating their contract with the estate agent. They wished to move out of Bristol, near the sea because of Mrs E's knee cap problems. They wished to buy a bungalow instead. They were looking for £159K for the house. I explained the situation of the market and told them that many sellers are cutting the asking prices by £30K on average. I told them they should expect the same cut if they wanted to sell.

We talked for about thirty minutes and I left, promising a call with an offer within forty-eight hours.

I called back the second day with an offer of 25 per cent BMV, £119,962, to which they said no. I told them that I would keep in touch with them in the future.

The Accountant

I met my accountant at one of the networking events I signed up for in my local area, although at this stage, I had reduced the number of events I was attending. This one was brought to my attention by a friend of mine. So I groomed myself as usual and took my new glossy business cards with me. On them was my name with Property Investors as the title. Boy, I was proud and my confidence was high. When I got to the event, I saw that the proportion of tall leggy blonde-haired women to old men sipping champagne was high. During the first couple of hours there, I just networked as usual. Then I realised that the men I was approaching had no interest in talking business. Still, I just kept on looking for anyone who looked business-like. After some time, a woman plumber I was talking to remarked the same thing that I had noticed when I came in, and then it clicked! This was like a dating event, which explained why there were so many blonde women in the building. The old farts were looking to get laid while the blondes were looking for a sugar daddy for the night. I said to myself, well I am here now; I might as well just keep networking.

After some time, a man approached me and said that he had noticed my business card at the entrance. He introduced himself as an accountant and asked me if I had one yet. I told him I didn't but that I was looking for one. He gave me his card, he took mine, and he pointed out that he was at the event with a friend of his who was also a property Investor. He introduced me to RB. I later on discovered that he had forty-five properties in Bristol. The accountant had the right connection, and so he was hired.

During this stage in my development, I was also a member of several property forums where I had access to years and years of debates and topics. I would read threads for hours, I would study other investors' ways of thinking and I knew each poster as if he or she were my personal mentor. SingingPig and Property Tribe were a couple of these forums. I found a few quotes, which I would like to share with you on these forums:

"What does not kill you is not important."

"If you do not feel embarrassed by your offer, you are probably offering too much"; a SingingPig quote.

For me, I was doing many things but still was not doing enough. I needed to accelerate my knowledge even more, so I started to email and contact the people who were posting on these forums. They were all very helpful. I was cramming more things into my day; I decided to compile a daily recap for this book.

3 August 2010

I received a call from Julie R from Haart estate agency. She wanted to hear my offer regarding the property at Grove Park Terrace. I did not make any offer because the owner seemed to be determined to sell for at least £90K, which I was not prepared to offer. I told Julie R my impressions but she urged me and assured me that the vendor needed to sell and would take £85K.

I told Julie that I would send her an email the following day with my offer. She mentioned two other properties she had on her books within my price range.

Ines and I were leafleting in the BS5 area where Connolls estate agency showed me a property the week before. It was a repossession area so I thought I should target it particularly myself.

Our first thirty minutes were very embarrassing. We felt that we should not be doing this, but I kept saying to myself, the most boring stuff gives the biggest yield to any company. I read this on the SingingPig forum. We distributed over 200 leaflets in three hours, and then came the rain and we had to pack up and leave. As we were moving towards my car, I received a call from a woman asking if we would buy her two-bedroom house. Another call was from Mr E of Maldowers Lane. DIY did work!

4 August 2010

Today I spoke with Mr E, who resulted from my leafleting yesterday. He was very charming on the phone but appeared quite broke. He told me that if his phone should be cut, I should call him back as he has very little credit left. So I suggested I call him back straight away to save him the rest of his credit. Five minutes later, I called to arrange an appointment for the afternoon.

Our appointment was at 2.30 p.m. Of course, I was there fifteen minutes early just to get the feel of the area. I noticed that Mr E had a massive garage attached to his property, which was a semi-detached property. I remembered very well sliding a leaflet inside this brown wooden door yesterday thinking to myself, why in hell would anyone not change this old door! Little did I know then that he was going to call me. Anyway, after my observations of the property, Mr E arrived in his old banger. "Hi, you are early!" he said; to which I replied, "I am always early; that is how I work".

He took out two round loaves of bread; I guess he was hoping to have a quick lunch before I arrived. He was wearing dirty jeans and a grey, washed-out T-shirt; he was a clean-shaven, rather handsome man.

We went into the house and as I imagined, it was a man's house: Old wooden flooring that could be restored to its former glory, and a big open-plan lounge, quite dirty, which led to the kitchen, bathroom, and garden. Upstairs were two double bedrooms and a single room. The single room was used by his little daughter when she came to visit him.

Mr E had been married twice, once thirteen years ago when he had purchased this property. He said he later had had to buy his ex out in order to keep it. He had his daughter through his second marriage. The daughter lived with her mum in Bristol.

Mr E explained to me that his property had been valued at 180K eighteen months ago; he also said that he understood the condition of the market, so he did not expect the same valuation today.

I asked him what sort of price he would be happy with; he said something in the line of 160K. I explained that the best thing would be to send in a surveyor, which would then enable me to put in an offer. He was very happy with that.

I dropped the property conversation and moved on to his reason for selling. He said he wanted to travel round the world and set up a biking business away from Bristol. I asked how quickly he was planning to do that; he said anytime. He said he was not in a hurry. We spoke a little more and left after about thirty minutes of chatting. While walking me out, I noticed a bike parked close to his garage. I enquired a bit more, being nosey; he said it was a new purchase of his bought for £3,000. I complimented him on his good buy, shook hands again, and left.

I went home straight away and posted the deal on a property forum and also sent an email to my mentor, James S.

My intention for this property was to sell this deal to a developer for around £6K-£8K.

I sent an email to Julie R regarding Grove Park Terrace offering £70K, thinking this would never be accepted. This offer represents 30 per cent BMV. I felt so embarrassed by this offer that it took me a good dose of courage to send it.

I read on SingingPig that, "if you don't feel embarrassed by your offer, you are probably paying too much" so I stuck to my guns and sent the email.

5 August 2010

I went to the Bristol City Council website to research 2 Maldowers Lane and to see what the planning permission said regarding the redevelopment possibility of the garage. He had permission to build a two-storey building and to extend the roof further up.

I received a call from James S, my mentor, who told me that I always have the knack of attracting complicated deals. He asked me about the planning permission, to which I answered all was in order. He said that it looked very good and that it was a winner.

I contacted Mr E to arrange an appointment for a surveyor to come in, to which he agreed a day the following week.

I called Joy from Fast Surveyors to book in a survey. I use them as they are efficient and cheap, just £175 compared to £350-£400 others charge.

Joy asked me for the details via email, which I sent immediately.

I received an email from Julie R. I was too scared to open it, thinking she would insult me due to my very corky offer. I left it to settle in. I intend to open it later tonight.

I Leafleted in Fishponds with Ines. The last batch was so successful so we are doing this again.

I opened Julie R's email, which read, "Hi Taiwo, leave that with me; I'll speak with the vendor".

I just couldn't believe my eyes; she did not insult me! The estate agents must be rather keen to sell then.

6 August 2010

Joy from Fast surveyors emailed me to tell me the price of the survey: £350 plus VAT! I asked why such a high rate? She answered because of the land, and the planning permit on the property makes it more expensive. The surveyor would need to do more research.

I painfully paid with my credit card. I must make money out of this deal.

I received a call from Julie R the EA. She told me she tried her best to get my £70K offer through. She said the vendor had some debt against the property, which does not enable her to sell at such a low price. She then asked me if £70K was my maximum limit, to which I replied certainly not. I would put in the right offer on any property. I told her about the 2 Maldowers Lane deal and she immediately replied that she has a similar property in Fishponds for around £149K. This gives me an idea of how much I should offer Mr E then.

Julie R asked me to give her a buzz tomorrow to schedule a viewing. I shall do so as soon as I get back to Bristol.

9 August 2010

At the office, I called Julie R for an update on the property we spoke about on Friday. She was not there. Monday mornings are always a bad time to call an EA, in general; this is when they catch up on emails, calls, and the Saturday activities. I decided to call her back the following day instead.

I dropped Ines off in Fishponds this morning. The weather was looking very good so I decided to give her a head start while I went to the office to sort out some things. My idea was to join her around 2 p.m. to continue leafleting. She called me around 12.30 p.m. to tell me she had finished all her leaflets; she had had about 200 this morning. I was glad to hear that!

I joined her roughly around 1.30 p.m. with more leaflets. We had worked for about two hours when the rain started to sprinkle. Whilst working, we saw others doing the same thing as us. Amongst them were two little girls distributing pizza delivery leaflets. They were no more than seven to eight years of age. Then we saw an elderly man distributing newspapers. This motivated us even more to continue despite the showers getting stronger by the step.

After three hours of relentless rain, we decided to use a tree as cover until it stopped. Well, it didn't! And we didn't have an umbrella.

Ines had been walking since 9 a.m. and her ankles were hurting so I decided to call it a day. I asked what she would like as a treat that evening, to which she replied Ben and Jerry's cookie dough ice cream. We went to get a tub and off we went back home. I was so proud of her!

10 August 2010

I called Julie R regarding the property about which we had spoken. She gave me the addresses for two properties. One was 48 Forest Av, BS16, which was on the market for £149,950, and the other was 1 Elmcroft Crescent, a three-bedroom semi-detached with some land attached, BS7, which was on the market for £195K. She mentioned that the property had been on the market for quite some time and that the couple was getting a divorce and needed a quick sale. As part of my due diligence, I went straight to www.Rightmove.co.uk to check it out. It was on the market with multiple agencies such as Besley Hill, CJ Holes, and Connells. This is an indication of the need to sell quickly. Julie R also expressed the vendor's flexibility to sell for £190K.

I arranged for a viewing for this afternoon but Julie was unable to get hold of the vendors. I will have to wait till I get back from London then.

11 August 2010

Today I emailed Rory regarding the possibility of doing an assisted deposit on 2 Maldowers Lane. He texted me back via his Blackberry as he was in the south of France. His assistant in his UK office emailed me the structured deal guide. I will be looking to follow this strategy.

I received a private message from Jay Patel from a property forum; he had read my posting regarding selling a property with land attached. He said he might be able to put me in touch with some developers and do the deal either as a Joint Venture or as a lead sale. That sounded interesting as I might package and make a few thousands out of it. I called Jay immediately and we spoke for half an hour. I learned that he used to be a property developer as well but decided it was not for him. He now has an invention on which he is now focusing his attention. He also gives lease option courses.

12 August 2010

I called Jay for the second time; he explained the strategy he would recommend for 2 Maldowers Lane, that is LO. We spoke about all the possible strategies including delayed completion, LO and assisted deposit. He asked me about my negotiation skills, and I replied that they were okay but could be improved. I suggested he come with me for my meeting with Mr E of Maldowers Lane. He agreed to come over to Bristol the week of 25 August. My Monday meeting with him would be about finding out what he wants.

13 August 2010

I have a meeting with Julie R to view 1 Elm Crescent, a three-bedroom property with some land.

I had my second meeting with Mr E of Maldowers Lane.

16 August 2010

Today I dropped Ines off at Fishponds; the weather is going to be good. She took around 500 leaflets with her for the day. To my surprise once again, she finished within three hours. To my surprise, I received a phone call from a potential seller, called Georgina. We spoke briefly and we arranged a viewing for tomorrow at 10.30 a.m.

My friend Marie called earlier this morning to let me know she was ill and that I should check on her regularly just in case something happens. I went to see her after dropping of Ines; she was very ill, throwing up, shaking, and experiencing hot flushes. I thought she was going to die on me! I called the doctor who asked me to pick up a suppository prescription, which she had to take in order to stop the vomiting. My appointment with Julie R at 1.30 p.m. loomed ahead. I had to pick up Ines as she had finished distributing her leaflets; time seemed to be passing by so quickly I could barely think straight.

I rushed to get Ines, whom I couldn't find because her phone had ran out of juice; she couldn't call me because she had just used her last penny to call me earlier. At 1 p.m., we were still looking for one another. I decided to dash to my viewing appointment with Julie R and come back later for her.

I arrived at 1 Elmcroft Crescent just on time. Mrs Valerie, the vendor, took me in whilst I waited for Julie. I was introduced to her husband and son. Julie arrived and took over the viewing. The house was a big three-bedroom property with the potential of being a four-bedroom if the loft were converted. The stairs to the loft were already well in place which makes it very convenient. The property was very clean, well-kept, and bright. There was some land next to it, which gave it good development potential.

The asking price was £217K but negotiable to £190K. I noticed that the property was listed with several agencies; this is an indicator of how desperate the vendor is to sell the property.

I will work out the figures and put in an offer in a couple of days.

After my meeting, I went back to search for Ines, I finally found her sitting at Morrisons supermarket, starving and tired. I told her I had been looking for her since she had called me two hours earlier. I told her about the phone call from Georgina; she was so excited that her work was paying off.

Appointment with 2 Maldowers Lane

My second appointment with Mr E went moderately well. He was very confident because the surveyor I had sent apparently had told him his house was worth £200K. His cockiness made my offer of £140K sound quite ridiculous. He again stated that he was not so needy. He believed his house was worth a lot more. The surveyor's report showed it worth £165K after spending £12K to renovate the property, but Mr E would have none of it. I was prepared to pay only £20K for the land and £120 for the house.

I suggested the idea of sharing the profit once the plot was used to build two two-bedroom apartments. He refused and said he wanted a clean deal. I could go back to him later with a firm offer. He could take it or leave it.

I went back to Marie's house where Ines had been caring for her. We remained there until another friend came to take over at 8 p.m.

I emailed the 2 Maldowers lane surveyor's report to Jay Patel so he could have a look and advise me.

17 August 2010

The weather started off quite bad so I told Ines to stay at home whilst I went to my various appointments and to the office. I popped in briefly to see Marie; she felt a lot better and could now eat properly, thanks to the suppositories.

I went off to my 10.30 a.m. appointment with Georgina. I was fifteen minutes early, as always. Georgina's boyfriend, I think he was, opened the door. The property was a three-bedroom house in need of some minor repairs that would probably cost £7K. The big conservatory was quite impressive. New combo boiler and radiators had recently been installed. She and her husband had bought the property thirteen years ago. She had had to remortgage the house to pay off all the debts secured against the house. She told me the bank had nearly repossessed it two years ago while going through the divorce. She wanted to keep the property because of her three children. The remortgage was for £180K. The house is not worth even that in today's market. The first strategy that came to my mind was the lease option.

Georgina wants to move to a smaller place, her mind seemed fixed on Bovis Homes, a brand new development. I introduced the idea of lease option and we spoke about the falling market. She told me that in 2007, the house was valued at £210K, which was why she was able to remortgage at £180K. She seemed to be fed up with the house and eager to move on. I will reintroduce the idea of a lease option to her again.

I just received a reply back from Jay Patel telling me that this was a crazy deal and that I should call him as soon as possible for his "undivided attention". It sounds as if I could sell the lead to him.

Simultaneously, I received a call from a certain Mr Haeger who owns a property in Barton Hill, a two-bedroom house bought in 2004. I arranged to meet him today at 5.30 p.m. Fingers crossed.

My appointment with Mr Haeger went well. Mr Haeger is from Bangladesh and owns three other properties in Barton Hill area. He has a two-bedroom, a three-bedroom, and a four-bedroom. He hopes to sell the 2—and three-bedroom properties, buy another in Manchester, and rent out the four-bedroom in which he lives in at the moment with his family.

He showed me the two-bedroom as listed on the agency book with which he had just signed. He was asking for £150K. The agency listed it for £140K, and as soon as he showed me the pictures, I knew he was far too optimistic. His two-bedroom is worth at the very best £100K.

We made our move to the house, which was just a minute or two from his house. He had been renting it out to students for many years and he was just fed up with having to chase after his rent every month. He now has a family from Kurdistan in it. The two-bedroom is in a dire state. The kitchen needs to be updated, the bathroom too and all the walls and flooring redecorated. The total cost for the update would be in the region of £5K minimum. I told him I could do some research and get back to him the following day.

I spoke with Jay regarding 2 Maldowers Lane. I thought I would just try other strategies; I did not feel like collaborating with him. I decided to pull the plug the following day: too much talk, not enough action. He was probably just bluffing his way through the business.

18 August 2010

Today I joined the Property Tribe community through a recommendation on SingingPig. This site seems to be more mature, more egocentric, and more focused than many other property forums. I think I could learn quite a lot.

I posted yesterday the sale of Maldowers Lane plot on SingingPig and another website where lands can be sold. I got interest through SingingPig from R. Greensland, another investor in Bristol asking for the postcode. I will be speaking with him tonight at 6 p.m.

I have an appointment tonight at 5.30 p.m. with Mr Haeger to give him my offer. I prefer making my offers face-to-face rather than on the phone. Hopefully, he will realise that his house is not worth as much as he demands. My research shows that there is a similar two-bedroom on the same street, which is on the market for £119,950 and in much better condition, and a three-bedroom house, also in a much better condition and just a few seconds' walk from the location, which is on the market for £125,000. His house is not worth more than £100K. My initial offer would be £95K.

My meeting with Mr Haeger went as I thought it would. He expected too much for his house. I showed him comparables in his street, which were going for a lot less and which were in much better condition. I gave him my offer of 95K. His wife laughed, as she thought I was insulting their intelligence. I was firm and quick to make them understand that their property would not sell at the price they wished.

I told them to keep in touch in the future. I have the impression that they might later want me to manage their properties for them. They dropped a few hints. I am not that keen on the idea!

19 August 2010

I spoke with R. Greensland this morning regarding 1 Elm crescent and 2 Maldowers Lane. He said that the latter was not interesting because it would definitely cost around £160K to build a new home, which might only sell for £140K. On the other hand, he wants to see Elm Crescent, as a possibility for making greater profit might be there. It is in the area he knows well. We have therefore arranged a viewing for Monday 23.

This afternoon, my friend Marie called to ask me if I might be interested in managing her three-bedroom house for her and her sister's three-bedroom house for them. This could be an opportunity to start a letting agency in Bristol. I told her I would put some figures together and we would talk again next week.

I also received a call from another investor from a forum who might be interested in 8 Ridgway LO. I have taken all his questions and forwarded them to Georgina. Many routes are opening for me and I know that I have to be very cautious not to lose my head.

23 August 2010

I went to see Marie's mother, Mrs O, regarding the management of her children's houses. We spoke and she handed me the keys to a three-bedroom property in Beaumont Street in Bristol and another three-bedroom in Cheltenham. I was delighted as these were my very first management responsibilities.

She informed me that another letting agency has the keys as well but for some reason, they hadn't rented it out in two weeks. I knew I could let the place in a matter of days. So she told me whoever let it first would get the full management contract.

We visited the property and I could see that it needed a quick tidying up and cleaning too. As we were coming out, a neighbour approached us asking to view it for her friend. I proceeded to conduct my very first viewing experience. She was very impressed. She immediately told her friend to take the place. After the viewing, I told Mrs O that I would come back the following day to mow the lawn and do the cleaning. That very evening at about 7.30 p.m., I posted an advertisement on www.Gumtree. co.uk:

> Title: Three bedrooms! No agency fees! Five minutes
> to Cabot Circus!
>
> Letting information
>
> Date available: Now
>
> Furnishing: Furnished
>
> Letting type: Long term

A *modern* well-presented two-bedroom house situated minutes from Cabot Circus, *modern* fitted kitchen with white goods included, Good size lounge, separate diner leading to a bright and airy sun room. Bathroom with shower, two *double* bedrooms, boasting a low maintenance rear garden, *Furnished; available now.* Five minutes' walk to Cabot Circus shopping centre.

£650 per calendar month (pcm)

24 August 2010

I added four pictures to attract more readings.

Within hours, I had received over ten emails, and the following day calls just started coming in from 9 a.m. until the following morning. I think the title did the trick. I never understood why agencies have to charge the landlord and the tenants anyway. Why not just charge either the landlord or the tenant?

Mr Idoko was one of the first to call me that morning. He asked me if he could come over in the evening, to which I said yes, but also told him the flat might be gone by then due to the volume of response. He then asked me the time of my first appointment, to which I responded mid-day; in reality, my first was at 5 p.m. that day. He immediately cancelled his plans and made his way to the flat as I was leaving my house to clean the other house. He arrived as I was cutting the lawn.

He had a look and said he was going to take it. I asked for a holding deposit of £140 as a guarantee; he had cash so he gave it to me on the spot. We discussed his background a bit more and how many people would live there. It would be just him and his friend. I asked for a guarantor, ID, a NI number and all the documentation I learned from one of the property DVDs I had bought some time ago.

25 August 2010

I downloaded some letting forms from a property forum website and from Sally Lawson's website as guides to draft my contract with Mrs O and the tenants. I rewrote the downloaded documents in the name of STAK Rentals.

I will be charging Mrs O a £150 start-up fee plus 8 per cent commission for full management. This is 2 per cent cheaper than a letting agent's fee. I also do not charge the tenants any fees as opposed to letting agencies.

26 August 2010

I sent the entire contract to Mrs O and to Mr Idoko.

I visited Gumtree this evening looking for some private house sales. I came across three that might be very interesting. I called them to book appointments. One was with a property investor called Mike. He has a two-bedroom flat in Ducie Road, another was a studio flat, and the last was a two-bedroom house in Bedminster.

27 August 2010

I went to visit the two-bedroom in Ducie Road this morning. The owner, Mike, showed me around and told me that he had owned 500 units at one point of his investing career. He now focuses on the higher end of the spectrum in the south of France. He is selling all his leaseholds to keep just freeholds. He is asking £125K for his flat. We spoke for a while, as I had so many questions for him. He said that he wouldn't be offended by any offer I might make him. I will call him on Monday to make my offer.

On the same day, I received a text message from the seller in Bedminster; we arranged a viewing for Sunday 5 September.

Alex from JJFox called me, as my details had been passed on by the vendor of the studio flat. He arranged a viewing for Tuesday, 31 August at 10.30 a.m.

At 10 a.m., I set off for Cheltenham to visit Mrs O's second property. The trip took about fifty minutes. Her son, Abel, was waiting for me there to show me around. The house is a three-bedroom but is currently used as a four-bedroom student flat. The house is in dear need of attention. Many things were broken and the furniture needed replacing.

Mrs O wants to rent it to a family, but I think that for that to happen, she would need to spend at least £10-15K on repairs, and if she would like to get in students, £5k would need to be spent.

I told her that if she could get the money together, I could find workers that could turn the place around in a matter of weeks. She said she would let me know on Tuesday.

18 September 2010

Today I arrived at Swindon Road with my team of traders to refurbish the three-bedroom house. My painter-decorator came from London, my electrician and plumber from Bristol, and my flooring from Cheltenham.

My schedule to turn this place around is three weeks maximum. My painter-decorator had just two days to complete his job. Matt the plumber came to see the house for an estimate. The entire boiler system was to be changed which would cost around £2,500. The electricity was up-to-date but had to be licensed; this would cost roughly £240. The flooring needed to be changed completely. My budget was £1,000.

19 September 2010

Kal, the floor man came to show me samples. I chose vinyl wood imitation for the corridors, the reception, and the room downstairs, and fake marble imitation for the bathroom. Depending on the quote, I might do the three rooms upstairs or just leave them as they are.

I also considered changing the kitchen but the budget will not allow that.

Project management schedule

Job	Interior refurbishment cost
Address	209 Swindon Road, Cheltenham

Job	Standard Costs in £: 3-Bedroom House	Budget
Kitchen inclusive of flooring	1,500	
W/C	250	
Bathroom	1,000	
Painting inclusive of materials and labour	1,000	700
Flooring inclusive of materials and labour	1,000	1,000
Boiler	2,500	2,000
Garden	100	
Guttering repairs	500	400
Project management	1,700	1,000
Rewiring or changing of fuse box / certificate	1,000	240
Allow 15% contingency		

My painter-decorator did his work in two days as planned; I paid him and he left for London on Monday 20.

During this week, I returned excess paint bought from B&Q to minimise my expenses on the project.

29 September 2010

The following Wednesday, 29 September, I brought to Cheltenham the plumber, the floor technician, and my electrician, whose duty was to update the electrics and issue a new safety certificate.

The plumber, Matt came with an assistant called Mark. Kal, the floor technician, came with two assistants, William and Chris. The job was to be completed in two days. Towards the end of the first day, the plumbers took out the old boiler, which was unfit for use in human habitation as it was discharging carbon monoxide. As they were preparing the wall for the new Worcester boiler, they came across a huge problem; there was a metal beam where they should create a hole in the wall. The only solution was to move the location of the boiler to the bathroom cupboard, upstairs. This meant that more-extensive plumbing work had to be done. This added a day of work and delayed the floor technicians from completing the bathroom floor. Pipe work had to be done under the bathroom floor. This obstacle also added costs to the whole project: £650 to the initial quote, £40 to tile and cement the old location, and £19.06 for tilling materials.

The landlord was not happy.

October-November 2010

4 October 2010

Kal came back to finish the floor as he had been delayed by the plumbers on Friday. The house looked sparkling new, smelled fresh, and looked fresh too. The landlord now had the tools to sell or rent the property fast.

5 October 2010

I received the final invoices from all my tradesmen, which I then passed onto the landlord. The final bill looked like this:

Job: Refurbishment of interiors

Address: 209 Swindon Road, Cheltenham

Job	Exact price	Description
Painting inclusive of materials and labour	650.40	Dirty walls; gave a cleaner look to the house
Flooring inclusive of materials and labour	1,450.00	The green carpet was the main reason all students turned the house away
Boiler	3,297.00	Emitted carbon monoxide and was unsafe for human habitation. No power flush included.
Tiling	40.00	
Guttering repairs		Requested by the landlord. To be moved to the back of the house. Price to be confirmed.
Project management	800.00	Inclusive of work done on the property, my time
Use of my car for shopping around for materials	200.00	The use of my car, quotes, etc.
Safety check update for electricity	120.00	There was no need to rewire but the safety check was out of date.
Electrician 1st visit	40.00	
Total	6597.80	
Advance received	1,500.00	On Friday 17 September
Remaining to be paid	5,098.00	

Later that evening, I set off to Peterborough for my first VIP millionaires meeting. I had joined this club of highly motivated property investors to keep me close to the fire. Being in Bristol, I felt lonely and unable to progress as I wished in the property business.

When I got to the office of my Duo gurus, it was bigger than I had thought. I introduced myself to the group of fifteen investors; some were novices, some were more experienced.

Rory presented different creative ways to finance deals. I had known those strategies before, but it was refreshing to hear them again. After the meeting, I had my one-to-one meeting with Trev and Jill, last year's VIP team members. I was given a few tasks for the following month's meeting.

Trev specialises in lease options and he explained to me how it works, but I was not very keen on using this strategy. He recommended I read a book called *How to Create Multiple Streams of Income* by Peter Conti and David Finkel

I was asked by Trev where I wished to invest and I told him that I was considering Newport, South Wales where the yields are far better than in Bristol. He gave me a task to see four estate agents and view eight properties before the next meeting. He told me to ask the EAs where *not to* invest in Newport. My task was to head off to Newport in a week or so to start my mission.

6 October 2010

I ordered *How to Create Multiple Streams of Income* on Amazon. My task was to read it for my next VIP meeting.

7 October 2010

Kal kept ringing me from 9.30 a.m. for his money. I was hopeful the landlord had transferred a part of the money this morning so I paid him straight away. He was an ass and I don't think I will use him again.

I was not sure if managing other people's property was the way forward for me. It took too much of my time for very little reward. This was something to keep an eye on.

10 October 2010

I was now using my credit card to support myself. I only needed £800 per month to cover my very cheap lifestyle; £650 went towards my mortgage and the rest was for the bills and food. Then I had an idea. Why not rent out two rooms in my house and create some passive income?

I called a couple of letting agencies and asked them if they did house share. Most of the ones in my area only take on whole properties. So I decided to move out of my three-bedroom house and go to London to live in a house share. At this stage, I was planning to return to part time work in London and keep doing my property things remotely. I would come to Bristol whenever I needed to and stay at a friend's house for a couple of days.

11 October 2010

I gave my house to two agencies, Greenwoods and Smartmove. Greenwoods put a letting board in front of my house and the visits started pouring in. They decided to market the entire house for £695; I told them that I wanted £725 because of the standard of the house and because it was going to be fully furnished. I had nowhere to store all my white goods and furniture. After about two days, I had received several offers. Then three Italian men came to view the house. They were early so I let them in instead of waiting outside in the cold for the letting agent to show them around. We got to talking and I told them that I had had many offers already and I was reluctant to let my beautiful house to three men. They wanted the house so badly they told me they would pay me £1000 pcm for it. I swallowed my tongue, took their number, and asked them to come back after the agent had gone. So the agent came and went and the three men came back. I told them I needed a month's deposit and a month's rent. They brought that to me the following day. Within twenty-four hours, I went from having no money to having £1000 in cash in my hands. They told me they needed to move in within twenty-four hours because their hotel was costing them a fortune. I asked for a week, we settled on three days.

13 October 2010

I called my mother and we moved all my stuff into the garage. Off I went to live in London knowing that my house would not be repossessed.

After three weeks of living in London, I thought to myself, what if I could do this again? What if I could take over a property from a struggling landlord such as I had been, let each room, pay the landlord a monthly rent that covered the mortgage, and give him or her the same peace of mind I was given when the three Italians walked through my door? I toyed with the idea for several nights. Then I became friendly with the manager of the house share in which I was living in London. I asked him who the landlord was and how many properties he had. He gave me some information, which I digested for several nights. I then went back to him and asked him if the landlord owned all the properties on his books; he said yes. Then I asked, what if he didn't own them, would that be illegal? He said no. He was managing the houses for the landlord, so his profession could not be illegal. Then the light bulb went on!

10 November 2010

My tenants contacted me to ask if I had a bigger house because one of their friends was coming to join them and they needed more space. As I already had the tenants, I decided to give it a go to find a four-bedroom house for them. I asked them if they wanted to stay in my area or wanted to be closer to the city centre; they chose the city centre, so I went on to contact all the agents near the centre.

It was time for me to fake it again. So I put on my big girl voice and started calling the agents. Many said no to my requests; some asked me for information I couldn't provide. Then I changed my script. I was now an international representative working with foreign companies relocating to Bristol. I was in charge of accommodation. I had to find accommodation for international executives moving to Bristol. The story worked. I got to do some viewings; but there was not enough profit to make a deal worthwhile. I was looking to make at least £500 profit on each property.

13 November 2010

I found an advertisement on Gumtree. It was a four-bedroom house ten minutes by bus from the centre for £800 pcm. I contacted the agent, she showed me around, and I asked her how long the property had been empty. She said six months. I immediately reduced my offer to £700 pcm; we settled on £725. I told her I needed to move in within two days. I gave her my card number there and then to secure the house, and I moved my Italian tenants in two days after. I moved back into my house. I had a business. This was my light bulb.

Here is the breakdown of the figures:

Rent of house: £725

Room 1: £375

Room 2: £375

Room 3: £375

Room 4: £375

Total gross income: £1,500

Bills (Council Tax, water, TV licence, broadband): £208

Net profit: £567pcm passive income

I could not believe it.

16 November 2010

I contacted the same agent to ask if she had any other houses available; the answer was yes. I immediately took my second house from her for £750, then another for £700, then another for £700. Between November 2010 and February 2011, I had four houses with this agent and two others with another agent. I was clearing £3,000 pcm in passive income. I was financially free. I was financially stable within three months. I had found a niche business model by accident and it worked. I was helping struggling landlords, and I was also helping foreigners who would never pass any letting agents' criteria. I had a business in a box.

Chapter II

THE DISCOVERY

Perfecting the system

Rent2Rent: It is what I call solving the problems of landlord and tenant in one go. There are many accidental landlords out there. Some people have inherited an estate: they wish to keep it but do not have a clue how to maximise profit. Others become easily discouraged as landlords as soon as they hit the wall of bad tenants. On the other hand, young professionals are dying to climb on the property ladder. These people often come out of university crippled with debt, which they have to pay off gradually. Often, they do not wish to continue living in student accommodations. This is where my strategy comes into play. As I said earlier, I solve two problems at once: I take the landlord's property on a long term rental agreement (an assured shorthold tenancy agreement) and I multi-let it to a young professional (licence to occupy) for a short period of time, three to six months. The profit in the middle is mine to keep.

The landlord gets paid every month for the period of our agreement—I take away his pain; the tenant gets a comfortable accommodation for the period of our agreement—I take away his pain also. The mortgage lender is happy because the landlord pays on time every month. The tenant is happy because he gets to save enough money to get on the property ladder.

Taiwo Orishayomi
Rent2Rent

About Me

Taiwo: Background: Ex publisher, Advertising, Marketing.

What you will learn today

- How to invest in Property without having vast amounts of cash as deposits.
- How to get into property Investing for less than £4,000 start up capital.
- How to gain control of a property for Corporate Letting.
- How to make up to 100% ROI from a property you do not even own.
- How to create a **"Passive Income Stream"** from Corporate Letting.

Key Point 1

- How to locate your own Goldmine Rental Area.
- How to Test Drive your area for rental demand.

Key Point 2

- How you can research Rental Income on the web.
- How you can calculate the "**Potential**" rental profit before contacting the Landlord/Owner.

Key Point 3

- How to find Landlords/ Private Owners.
- How to take control of the property without committing to buy it.

Key Point 4

How to best advertise your rooms to let using social media.

Other Portals

- www.Gumtree.co.uk
- www.spareroom.co.uk
- www.easyroommate.co.uk
- www.flatshare.co.uk

Key Point 5

- Signing the contract and Legals with the renter.
- DPS, Mydeposit.

What not to do

- Don't Invest in the wrong areas ie:
- No shops
- No public transport
- No Corporate employers.
- No facilities, Universities, etc.....

- **Location, Location, Location is everything.**

What to do

Research, Research, Research thoroughly the area you wish to invest in.
1-3 postcodes is enough.

Case study 1

Kimberley Rd
- Landlord rent: £700pcm
- Bills (council tax, water, TV licence, Broadband, Cleaner): £208pcm
- Room1: £385pcm
- Room 2: £385pcm
- Room 3: £375pcm
- Room 4: £320pcm
- Gross income: £1,465
- **Net Profit per month: £557**

Case study 2

- **Lodge**
- Landlord rent: £700pcm
- Bills (council tax, water, TV licence, Broadband, Cleaner): £208pcm
- Room1: £360pcm
- Room 2: £360pcm
- Room 3: £325pcm
- Room 4: £320pcm
- Room 5: £306pcm
- Gross income: £1,671
- **Net Profit per month: £763pcm**

Case study 3

- **Douglas**
- Landlord rent: £795pcm
- Bills (council tax, water, TV licence, Broadband, Cleaner): £208pcm
- Room1: £375pcm
- Room 2: £350pcm
- Room 3: £350pcm
- Room 4: £350pcm
- Room 5: £350pcm
- Room 6: £330pcm
- Gross income: £2,105
- **Net Profit per month: £1,102pcm**

Case study 4

- Landlord rent: £1,100pcm
- Bills (council tax, water, TV licence, Broadband, Cleaner): £208pcm
- Room1: £475pcm
- Room 2: £465pcm
- Room 3: £450pcm
- Room 4: £375pcm
- Room 5: £360pcm
- Room 6: £350pcm
- Room 7: £330pcm
- Room 8: £220pcm
- Gross income: £3,025
- **Net Profit per month: £1,717pcm**

Kimberly Rd

Course Summary

- Multi-let, HMO or House Share
- Register Company Name or a Sole Trader (www.duport.co.uk)
- Websites and Business Cards: Look Professional
- Using www.bitly.com to shorten links
- Locate your highest yielding postcodes
- Locating the Property
- Working with Letting Agents
- View the Property: What to watch out for
- How to secure the Property
- How to advertise your rooms
- Using the social media to find tenants
- What to do when you pick up the keys
- Refurbishment: How much should you spend?
- Staging the Property: where to find cheap furniture?
- The Tenants: Which profile?
- Legal Requirements: AST, Deposit & Inventory
- Managing the Property: Notices
- Housekeeping
- How to Systemize your business from the start: house references, email communication, tenant spreadsheet
- How to handle bad tenant's
- Building Your Business
- Set Yourself A Goal
- Rent2Rent Full legal workbook

This is the system I have been using since I took on my very first property back in November. By the time I got my third property, I had more or less perfected it. Here are a few real life processes I went through (Properties 3 and 4).

Property 3: BRE37

I found this through a local letting agent, through www.Rightmove. co.uk to be precise. Yes, most of my houses at this stage were found either through www.Gumtree.co.uk or www.Righmove.co.uk. I read somewhere today that there are over 880,000 houses listed on www.Rightmove.co.uk. That is a goldmine in itself. This is a tool not to be dismissed in either buying or renting a property to rent.

I called the agent to arrange a viewing for the same day, as the price was just right. I had done my due diligence and I knew that a five-bedroom house in that area would be rented quickly to students, young professionals, or the large Polish community in that area. My targets here were postgraduate students—almost professionals. I was not too picky at this early stage.

I also did my figures:

The house was advertised for £895 pcm. I had to get it for £700 pcm, max. If my offer were accepted, which I knew it would be because of the time of the year, December, my figures would look like this:

Room 1: £385

Room 2: £360

Room 3: £310

Room 4: £300

Room 5: £300

Gross profit: £1,655

Rent: £700

Council Tax: £130

Water: £35

Internet: £30

TV licence: £13

Cleaner: £28

Total expenditure: £935

Monthly net profit: £719

Yearly net profit: £8,628

With these figures in mind, I scheduled a viewing for that very afternoon. The agent was quite surprised that I was so keen. I thought that would work against me in terms of negotiation. I am a big believer in taking action immediately. If you do not, someone else might come along and take the deal right from under your nose.

So, I got to the house fifteen minutes early, a rule of thumb in my books, just to take a look around. According to my satellite navigation system, the university was just a ten-minute walk away; there were two big supermarkets nearby, Morrisons and Lidl. Never under estimate Lidl: The food is cheap and many Eastern Europeans shop there. This is a good reason for choosing an area. There were also many Polish shops; again, a very good signal. The agent arrived on time. I took a look at the house: it was perfect. The house needed updating as it had been empty for quite a while. The grass was overgrown, bags of rubbish had been dumped in the garden by the previous tenants, and there was mould in the bathroom. This type of things would put off any tenant. The thing is, it would take me less than an hour to clear that out. A spray of bleach to kill off the mould, weed killer, and a bit of light cleaning would do the trick. I asked the agent the price again; she looked at her notepad and said £895. I asked if the landlord would be willing to negotiate. Surprisingly, she said yes. He would go down to £800. I needed to get her down to £700. In my head, I had already banked the £719 calculated profit.

Then I asked if the landlord would be willing to let it to me on a long term basis; by that I meant three years. The agent was rather shocked, but offered a smile. She was rather happy to hear that because I think they may have found it hard to rent every year. So with that information, I asked her to put forward my offer of £700. She made a phone call and came back with a yes. I should have offered £650, I said to myself. I asked the agent what the next step was. She asked me to pay a down payment of £200, which I did on the spot. I told her I needed to get the keys within the next forty-eight hours because my executives were arriving from France. I got the keys within twenty-four hours. The following day, I cleared the garden, cleaned the house, and put a deodoriser in each room to remove the stale smell of emptiness.

I went to Primark to get some bed linen just to prepare the rooms for pictures. The house was fully furnished, by the way. I took pictures, and they were online within hours. Two rooms were gone within the first week; the rest were gone within three weeks. That house has never been empty since. The same tenants are still in there almost a year later.

Property 4: FIL949

This property also came through a letting agent. It was taken on in February. The house was such a dump that no one in his or her right mind would dare take it on. I wonder why agents cannot be bothered to do some cleaning in order to rent out a house. Everything in the house was older than my mother. The furniture, cooker, fridge, even the carpet needed to be buried. Don't even get me started on the smell! Nevertheless when I saw the property, my hands started to sweat because all I could see was profit. Why? Because this house was just five minutes' walk to Airbus, one of the largest employers in Bristol. They have over 3,000 employees and many come from abroad. I knew I could grab tenants before they arrived in Bristol. Who would not want to be able to walk to work instead of sweating on the public transport?

The house was listed for £900. The figure I had in mind was closer to £700. All the furniture needed to be replaced at the landlord's expense, and the house must be managed by the agent not the landlord. I wouldn't want to get into a long-term partnership with a landlord who neglects his house. So I asked the agent to speak with the landlord; it was actually a landlady. Her response was very negative, so I told the agent that I was prepared to take the house for three years, meaning, *no void* during this term. She then opened up to negotiations with me. She asked for a list of things I wanted, which I provided immediately. Twenty-four hours later, she said she would do all of them within a week, but that some things would have to wait for the week after. I agreed. I then asked if the agent could take care of the management; she said no, but that I could handle that for her. If there were to be any repairs, I should just drop her an email to inform her and go ahead and sort it out; she would reimburse me. I agreed. We are now best of friends because she doesn't want to be bothered and I do not bother her. I pay her the rent on time every month and I make sure the house is immaculate inside out.

Here are the figures for the house. By the way, my offer of £700 was not accepted; I had to go up £50. The house was well worth £900.

Room 1: £400

Room 2: £400

Room 3: £360

Room 4: £300

Gross profit: £1,460

Rent: £750

Council Tax: £120

Water: £35

Internet: £30

TV licence: £13

Total expenditure: £976

Monthly net profit: £512

Yearly net profit: £6,144

Now, the profit on this one is quite low compared to what I was looking for, but the location allows me to increase the rent each time a new tenant moves in. I jack the price up by a fiver every four to five months.

I have to add here that although the house looked like a dump in the beginning, the old boiler and the central heating are reliable I have no problem with this house as I have with many modern houses.

Tenants: Managing My Properties

By now, I had six properties and twenty-six tenants to manage. One of the criteria I follow is not to look at anything less than a four-bedroom house or flat. There is no profit in a three-bedroom. Don't even think of a two-bedroom. As a rule, you want four bedrooms or more. When you get to five bedrooms, HMO rule comes into play, so you might want to check the rules with your local authority. Many landlords will work with you if you guide them. Most landlords I take on already have their licences in place, Bristol being a university area.

Also, bear in mind that this is a people business. You deal with the landlords, you deal with the agents, and you deal with your tenants, tenants being the most challenging part. The golden rule is to not allow tenants to control you. You control them. This rule has to be in place and understood right from the word go. Otherwise you will end up mothering them or being their slave.

Back to my day-to-day journal.

20 February 2011

I received a text message from one of my tenants saying that his housemate had attacked him. This is the same tenant who called me a week before about a noise in his room. It was the wind outside.

One problem about growing a property business of this type is the amount of paperwork that comes with it.

Setting up all utilities per house is a great pain but helps me be in control. No matter how much I complain, I still enjoy it.

21 February 2011

I started the day as usual by spending a few hours going through www.spareroom.co.uk and easyroommate.co.uk. I sent text messages to those with listed mobile phones.

I received a text from John to whom I had shown a single room in Horfield last week. He confirmed he would take the room. John is on the Department of Social Services list (DSS) so he has to inform the council and arrange the transfer of his payment to my account via a credit union account. At the same time, I received a call from Chelsea, a young woman looking for accommodation that welcomes DSS. As the two single rooms had been empty for over a week, I decided to take them on; they would stay and the council would pay.

I have an empty double room in Horfield in BOS71 and a single room in Fishponds in BRE37. I have an appointment tomorrow with Nikki, who is looking for a double room for her and her partner.

I received over four calls from potential tenants. My advertising and marketing are very consistent, calculated, and precise. This is the reason I always have viewings and my rooms tend to be rented most of the time.

22 February 2011

The phone rang at 7.45 a.m. with a call from Virgin Media. The installation of the Internet connection at the new house was planned for between 8 a.m. and 1 p.m. I was expecting them to arrive around 10 a.m. with at least one hour's notice. No, they called me at 7.45 a.m. to tell me they would be there within thirty minutes. I called one of the tenants to let them in. I'm glad I could rely on them.

I called Nikki to confirm our 12.30 p.m. viewing. Nikki is a Singaporean, and she came with a couple, her friends, who would be moving into the room.

I let them in and showed them around. They seem undecided, so I told them to think about it and to call me if they were interested. From there, I went to the LOD47 property, my only problematic property. LOD47 has five rooms and six tenants. A couple occupy one of the double rooms. For some reason, they just do not get along, nor do they even communicate. I have to come into this property at least once a week to resolve disputes among tenants. Anyway, my appointment was about the possibility of taking on a cleaner to clean the common areas of the house, as the tenants could not be bothered to do it.

My first appointment was with Rahmo, a Somalian woman. She charges £6 an hour. She looks very willing, and she lives just around the corner. My second appointment was with Rosksana, a Polish woman. She came with her daughter, as her English is not fluent enough. She charges £6.50 an hour.

I received so many responses from my www.Gumtree.co.uk advertisement that I had to pull it down within twenty-four hours. My dilemma was to decide which woman to hire. I wish I could employ both of them.

After my interviews, I popped in to BRE37 property, where the ceiling in one of the rooms had fallen off a week before. Everything was repaired and I needed to move the sitting room into where the formal room was and vice versa. Paul, one of the happy chappy tenants, was there to give me a helping hand. We dismantled some furniture; I pinched my fingers several times. The work was completed within an hour.

I went back home to check emails and work on my Bristol rentals website. At this stage, I had so many rooms that I decided to have my own niche website for my growing mailing list of potential tenants. I would put pictures and details of each property there, so I wouldn't have to keep answering the same questions from tenants.

23 February 2011

My day started at 6.30 a.m.; I stayed in bed and read a chapter of *House Share Super Hero by Steve Julien*, which was given to me by Jason, a guy I was helping out in my rental strategy. The book was all right; it gave some tips and reminded me of others; however, the strategy was outdated and could not be adapted to today's market. Good read though.

At 9.30 a.m., I confirmed all my viewings to make sure I did not waste my time. I had two viewings planned and I had one unexpected, which was altogether good.

At 12.30 p.m., I had an appointment with GM, a letting agent, concerning a property I was interested in. The property was a five-bedroom house not far from another one I have; £795 pcm, and a good deal. The state of the house was horrendous but once the current tenants leave and the whole house is washed out, it will be a good bargain. I will get the keys in June. I know: early birds. Sometimes when a bargain comes up, just take it. Lady Luck might not come by twice.

Back home, paid my reservation fee of £200 by phone and posted my new ad on Gumtree and easyroommate. I caught up with Frank and Janet Wolley, some of my property friends. They've just got back from Egypt.

Tomorrow, I deal with the paperwork.

24 February 2011

My day started as usual at 6.30 a.m. with a chapter of the book I was reading at the moment. I spent an hour on emails and updating advertisements and then moved on to some invoices. I also arranged direct debits for utilities and opened some letters. This took me another one hour.

My first appointment was with Jose, a Spanish guy who contacted me previous night through my ad on Gumtree. Jose had just arrived and he started working the next day with Aardman, the company that produces animated films such as *Wallace and Gromit* and *Chicken Run*. Jose looked very shy but very organised. He saw the room in Fishponds and took it straight away. He paid his deposit and first month rent in cash. I showed him where the shops were in the area where the house was and dropped him off at the city centre so he could set up my standing order with his bank.

I met Roksana, my new cleaner for Fishponds. I took all her details, asked what she would need for the cleaning, and arranged a start date for the following Tuesday.

I met Julien, a friend of mine who is also self-employed. We met to organise our first networking event with the FSB (Federation of Small Businesses). While we were together, I received two calls from potential tenants who wanted to view my double room in Horfield. Antonio and Jenny were given a 4.30 p.m. appointment at BOS9. They both showed up. Hopefully one of them will take the room.

I received a call also from one of my oldest tenants, Gilbert, who was looking to upgrade his room. He wanted to have his own facilities. I promised to come up with something soon.

I went back home for more emails, website updates and phone calls.

25 February 2011

My day started with a few pages of *House Share Hero*.

My first appointment of the day was with the Spanish couple who wanted a double urgently. It was their first viewing in Bristol. I was not keen on renting the small double to a couple; it was more suitable to a single person and ideally, a woman. They promised to give me a call later that day to give me a feedback on all their viewings but oddly, they never did. I wonder why every viewer says, "I'll let you know", or "I'll call you tomorrow with an answer", but never does.

I visited the BOS1 property, a similar house to the BOS9 property, which I currently have. The house was in such a mess that even squatters would refuse it. It was also a company let and the tenants had left without paying rent for three months and did a runner. The agency was asking for £1,200 pcm; this was negotiated down to £1,000 but still, the price was higher than that at number 9. I put in an offer of £800, which was rejected. The maximum I could pay was between £850 and £900, take it or leave it. We settled on £900.

My second appointment of the day was with Andreas, another Spanish man. The whole of Spain seems to be relocating to Bristol, in my opinion. Andreas already lived in Bristol; he was looking for a double room in my area. He did not seem very enthusiastic so he left.

At the end of the day, I received a text message from another Andrea, an elderly Canadian woman who I had just moved from another property to BOS9; she wanted her computer checked because of the ceiling accident that happened at the last address. Andrea tends to blame others for everything and she is the type that would milk any situation to the max. I had to be careful with every communication I had with her.

I finished my work at 3 p.m. I chilled for the rest of the day.

26 February 2011

Saturdays are usually fairly busy, with viewings spread over the entire day. My first viewing of the day was at 10 a.m.; I had others at 10.30, 11.00, and finally 1.30 p.m.

During my spare time between viewings, I roamed around the closest streets taking note of the "To Let" signs. I would contact them the following Monday. I would not mind controlling a few properties in the area.

27 February 2011

I try not to work on Sundays, but occasionally, I have to. I received a call this morning from the Spanish couple who had viewed the Horfield double room on Thursday. They desperately wanted to move in; I guessed their first choice had fallen apart. So I gave them an appointment for 1 p.m. They were there on time; we signed the contracts and they paid me £400 for the rent. The remaining £400 deposit would be paid on Tuesday, as they needed to change their Euros.

Good day!

28 February 2011

For me, a good day is when I have a rent payment deposited to my account; today, I had received four rental payments and one full deposit for another month. That is the beauty of the month of February.

On another note, two of my current tenants are not pulling their weight, meaning, they are late, and I have to keep up the pressure to put them straight. Paul, my tenant at BRE37, was expecting help from the council, but instead of informing me about the delay in his payment, he chose to keep quiet. Although I joke with him a times, I made him understand that when it comes to my rent, I do not banter. I went to see him unexpectedly and I asked him what was going on. He was surprised to see me, and he showed me all his council paperwork to prove that payment was coming soon.

My strategy is to put the pressure on all late payers at all times. One day late is already too late. My tenants will hear from me within twenty-four hours.

Lee is another tenant at BRE37. He is in his forties, and he has just started a new job. He had explained his situation to me right from the start so I have been flexible with his payments. Lee promised to make his full February month payment today, so when I did not see any bank transfer or hear from him, I sent him a text in the afternoon. When he heard me speaking with Paul, his next-door neighbour, about his delay, Lee quickly came out to tell me he was just about to withdraw cash for me. He asked me where he could find a cash machine; I told him at the supermarket. He went straight there and withdrew two-thirds of his rent, promising to pay the rest on Friday.

The Spanish couple at BOS9 paid the remainder of their deposit and we spoke for a while about their National Insurance card interview. I assured them it was not an interrogation, just a simple procedure. They were quite terrified of the whole thing because they were new in the country.

Part of being self-employed in the property industry is the amount of paperwork involved. So part of today was dedicated to my backlog.

March-June 2011

1 March 2011

Today was another good day: more cash in the bank and the late payers promised to make payment within few days. I went to a business exhibition with a friend of mine. There was nothing worthwhile but it was a good day to meet other business people.

2 March 2011

It was another hectic day, with a lot of driving around, making phone calls, meeting people, and sending emails. My day started at roughly the usual time. The first appointment was at 10 a.m. with a gentleman called Joska; a Hungarian name but English born and bred. Joska arrived with his dad; one could see straight away that he was a DSS, and he wouldn't stop calling me "love", a denominative that I hate. Joska is a young man and a heavy smoker, judging from the state of his teeth. I asked him to pay the first month deposit in order for me to accept his DSS case. I never heard from him again.

My second appointment was with John, a mature man looking to move but not in so much of a hurry. He had a look but did not express any urgency.

Then I received a call from the council regarding Ella, a young DSS girl. The council wanted to inspect the house to make sure it was secure enough to go ahead. We set a date and time for them to come over.

My new cleaner, Roksana, started today with the LOD47 and BRE37 houses. I might extend her services to the NEW61 house soon.

4 March 2011

Today, I had an early appointment with a gay couple who contacted me on Spareroom. They needed to move urgently because the one-bedroom flat they were previously supposed to move into had been withdrawn at the last minute because the landlord had found out they were gay. Aajay, the one who contacted me, came along with his partner and they viewed the house. I think it was not up to their expectations, but beggars can't be choosers, as they say. I explained to them that it did not bother me to have them there and it would not bother the other tenants either. Aajay called me back at 10.30 p.m. asking if he could move in.

I saw the man from the council today. He loved the house and asked me for three certificates in order to make the house rentable for their clients.

I needed a gas safety certificate, an EPC (Energy Performance Certificate) and a periodic inspection report. I asked GM if they had them, and they sent me the gas report and the EPC. I have to get the PIR done next week.

The council is a good safety net for any voids I may have. They apparently have hundreds of young people looking for rooms. They also said that they could move someone in within two days.

Patco, the man from whose shop I do my bulk photocopies, asked me to help him with one of his properties on Wells Road. You never know when offers will come along. I went to see the property and I told him that for me to take it on, it had to be made HMO compliant. I asked Graham, a GM handyman who is a friend, to become involved. He would be able to change the house to the GM standard; this would allow me to rent it out legally. This is part of my second term plan, which is to approach landlords directly about their properties.

This afternoon, I met Justin Phillips, the mortgage advisor introduced to me by the Wolleys. He came for lunch, which he paid for, bless him, and explained all my options in terms of getting into a buying spree once again. He said I could buy a small unit, for example a studio apartment, to get the ball rolling. Once that is done, I will be eligible for 80 per cent LTV with the banks. Justin Phillips used to be an estate agent and he has seventeen units himself. So I guess he knew what he was talking about. My homework now was to start searching for a studio flat under £50K.

5-6 March 2011

I went to the property super conference with Duo. As a crew member, my days started at 7.30 a.m. and ended at 9.30 p.m. The event was successful with a lot of networking possibilities. Lord Allan Sugar came for an hour's speech. The event was a way to update myself on mortgages, creative financing, deal packages, negotiations, auctions, and much more. Since I had started my Rent2Rent strategy, I had abandoned the other sides of the business.

This is a further motivation to be successful in my strategy.

Analysis of my strategy: This was my plan for the following four months.

Property	Rooms	Profit	
1	5	800	
2	5	800	
3	4	500	
4	4	500	
5	4	500	
6	4	500	
7	4	500	
8	5	800	
9	4	500	
10	4	500	Total:6,000

Save £15K to buy a small unit, studio under £50K, 75 per cent LTV in July

September: buy a bigger unit, three-bedroom, 80 per cent LTV, £20,000

December: buy my third unit, 80 per cent LTV, one-bedroom

My strategy was noticed by many of my investor colleagues and some were asking me to coach them. I am now toying with the idea of charging a standard fee for it, perhaps one-day training for a fee of £1,000. One day training a week, four days per month, £4,000 revenue. I sit with that idea for now.

8 March 2011

My day started at 6.30 a.m. because I had accumulated a bit of work after my weekend super conference absence.

I had over eighty emails to go through. It took me almost four hours to go through them.

I started a new advertisement on bristolrentals.wordpress.com, Spareroom. co.uk, and Easyroommate. This one was for the BOS1 house, which was being renovated by GM.

The advertisement is below.

> A large, newly decorated house just off Gloucester Rd has just become available. The house is very spacious. There are two very large double rooms, which can accommodate couples.
>
> Great Location
>
> The house comprises three large double bedrooms and a single room. The rooms are fully furnished.
>
> A lounge with sofas
>
> Fully furnished kitchen with washing machine/dryer
>
> Garden
>
> Free parking
>
> Most bills inclusive (Council Tax, water, TV licence, and fast wireless broadband)
>
> Gas and electricity are shared among tenants
>
> Weekly cleaner
>
> Double room 1: £455 pcm
>
> Double room 2:£435 pcm

Double room 3: £400 pcm

Single room: £300 pcm

If you feel that this might be a good environment for you, please contact me to arrange a viewing.

Kind regards,

Lauren

Lauren is my Internet name. I think that Taiwo sounds strange and might put people off. Lauren can be pronounced easily and is a name that exists in several languages.

Kumar from Patco, who wanted me to handle his four-bedroom house for him, called to confirm the appointment I had arranged with him and Graham, the GM handyman. We all met at the property; Graham did the tour and explained the regulations and the process of updating the house to an HMO standard. Kumar seemed to be very eager to get the ball rolling, as he did not want the void to be too long. Graham would get back to me with a quote.

I visited DOW14 and discovered that one of the tenants, Lloyd, had been damaging a few doors with his bike. I called him and asked him to repair the damages. He was not very happy about it. I am in contact with his parents, so if he ever proves difficult, they would be the first to know.

BRE37 was dirty as usual. The cleaner was due to come the following day. The tenants had hundreds of empty cans of beer in the pantry; I had sent a warning to clean up the mess.

BOS9 was clean as usual, but Andrea called again because she could not figure out how to use the washing machine. I showed her where the manual was.

One of my dreaded duties is the letters. I had over twenty to go through today. At least I am up-to-date with the bills.

Over 100 text messages were sent out today to inform potential tenants about the new house at BOS1. I also stated in the text that those who were no longer looking for accommodation should text back "no" to be removed from my mailing list. I got two *no*s out of 100. This was not bad!

9 March 2011

Today started with two hours of advertisement updating on Gumtree, Easyroommate, and Spareroom. I responded to all the emails and got a few interested in Saturday viewings. An elderly man from Germany called to get some more information about BOS1. He and his wife were planning to get down to Bristol in the next few weeks. I got another call from an older woman, Jo, who was coming for the viewing too.

The copy of the key made for my cleaner by Timpson was not working so I had to give her mine and make a new copy. The electrician booked to do my periodic inspection report did not show up, this delayed getting a DSS tenant in. After a full day of problem solving, I went to Bristol Pin where Jim Haliburton was speaking. Jim is the HMO daddy.

I am thinking about taking his courses and one-to-one training too. He made us an offer I could not refuse: a whole training package, cd, forms, and guide, for only £595. I took it.

11 March 2011

I signed my first LHA tenant today. He will be paying fortnightly via credit union account. His name is John Paul Goatley (with a little help, he could have been Gautier!), a young Englishman. One wonders how such a man could be unemployed when many foreigners arrive every day and get work. I kept my eye on him. Unfortunately for him, I could not keep him for long. He kept breaking my house rules.

I met with my accountant today regarding my books and insurances. Being in the property business, the HM revenue & Customs is prone to investigate my business, so he suggested I took investigation insurance just in case. I will be paying him £140 pcm, this includes:

Sole trading account, one hour per month: £50 plus £20 investigation insurance

Limited company account, one hour pcm: £50 plus £20 investigation insurance

This looks fair to me.

One of my problematic tenants has decided to leave; he gave me just a week's notice. I told him that he should find a replacement tenant or he would lose his deposit.

The number of tenants moving out this month was now four; I had to take just one property this month in order to keep afloat.

I went to visit BOS1 today to prepare for tomorrow's early bird viewings. I had sent emails to over 300 potential tenants and had texted over 200. I am expecting at least a dozen of people between 1 and 2 p.m.; hopefully all the rooms will be let as soon as possible.

I received a call from Geoff Whitiker, a fellow property contact who is interested in my business model. He wanted me to coach him, so he will be coming over to Bristol next week, on Wednesday, for a few hours of coaching. I seriously need to start thinking about charging for my time.

Tomorrow is another day.

12 March 2011

Today was my early-bird viewing. Five people came, two took rooms, and the other three left. The largest of the double rooms was taken by a Spanish father and daughter for a six-month contract, and the single room was taken by an Australian man. The Spanish people will move in the following day and the Australian on the twentieth.

I intended to let the remaining two rooms by the end of the week.

Another problematic tenant, Manu, has decided to ignore my calls and texts. Perhaps he has left the country. I will write a visit letter in order to gain access to his room. I hope he is fine.

14 March 2011

Manu still had not returned any of my calls; I am starting to get worried now. I will access his room tomorrow.

Two people got in touch with me via Gumtree. I showed them the house today.

Ella Tripp, the girl from the council, moved into her room today. Her case manager, Felicity, came to do the inventory and to sign all the necessary papers. Ella requested that her bed be removed as she had her own. I took the bed to my new Spanish father and daughter tenants at BOS1, as they needed it. I dismantled the bed and managed to fit it into my Puma car. That saved me £25!

As I was driving back home, I received a text from Esteban, my new Spanish tenant, requesting me to come back because the hot water wasn't working. I smiled; barely ten minutes later, he texted back saying that it was now working. I am not sure what these tenants think, perhaps that I am their poodle. Always leave twenty-four hours between the time they contact you and the time you visit the house, unless it is a life or death emergency. In most cases, they figure out the solutions themselves.

Andrea, my tenant from BOS9, had sent me a text a couple of weeks ago regarding the washing machine, and I had showed her how to read the manual. Then a few days later, she texted, requesting me to send someone to have a look. I ignored her altogether. Today, she emailed me, saying how glad she was to be in the property, and that she would like to extend her tenancy agreement.

Sam, my tenant at DOW14, called to complain about Lloyd, my most challenging tenant. Lloyd's parents had contacted me before he moved in. I think they were trying to get him away from them. Lloyd refused to respect the rules and regulations of the house; instead, he would invite his friends over for a good time. I noticed bike tyre marks on all the downstairs doors; these were left by Lloyd. I called him and requested them to be cleaned, but this was not done.

Sam's call was to inform me about the real state of the house. He informed me that Lloyd had had his girlfriend living with him for the past ten days, and that he had made a huge hole in his door, probably as a result of kicking it. I informed the rest of the tenants I was now in the process of evicting Lloyd and that it had to be done in the right way.

I sent a text to all tenants informing them of my routine house inspection, which would take place the following day. From there, I would have proofs of damages to the property and then involve Lloyd's parents.

15 March 2011

My days tend to start earlier and earlier while my nights tend to be shorter despite the return of the sun. By 7.30 p.m., I'm ready to go to bed.

This morning, my viewings started at 10.30 a.m. About two hours prior to this time, I texted my scheduled appointments asking for confirmation, as usual. The person I was to meet at 10:30 texted back but the person coming for my 10 a.m. appointment didn't, so I just prepared myself for the 10:30 viewing. While I was on my way, at about 9.50 a.m., the person for the appointment at 10 a.m. texted back confirming his viewing. I told him I would be a few minutes late, and shortly after that, the person for the 10.30 a.m. appointment texted to cancel. All worked out pretty well. The 10 a.m. got lost on the way, giving me time to get there. He came but he was looking for something closer to the town.

A few hours later, while I was enjoying the sun on Gloucester Road, I received a call from Aajay, a guy who had been in touch with me a few months back regarding the DOW14 property. He wanted to view the room now. I told him I could meet him in fifty minutes. He had the audacity to request a pick up from Dominos where he worked. I laughed and told him to find his way. I have now stopped being the Good Samaritan, especially because those for whom you go out of your way to help are the same people who often end up letting you down. I have learned my lesson.

So Ajay went to DOW14 and called me to say he was there. I told him that that house was already gone and that the new one, thankfully, was just fifteen minutes' walk away. He finally turned up with his wife, who I suspected was in the early stages of pregnancy. So I showed them the large room downstairs, focusing on the easy access to the kitchen and bathrooms and the fact that I had a weekly cleaner who comes to the house. I also mentioned Southmead Hospital just close by. They were quickly charmed by the whole thing. The house was also close to their work. Ajay later mentioned that the hospital was the key convincer. They took the room and would move in a month. I gave it to them for £400 pcm, providing they signed for six months.

I contacted Rory and Frank again regarding the b. & b. project; I was working on some figures and estimates, and by God's will, we could buy the property.

I was getting more and more worried about Manu, whom I hoped had not committed suicide. I would visit his room tomorrow.

I visited DOW14 for an inspection of the house and rooms. I had received a call the night before from two other tenants complaining about Lloyd Lawson. He decided that the house was his party ground. I had spoken with Lloyd a few weeks back as he was damaging the doors of the house with his bike. When I asked him to clean up the traces on the doors, he got angry and hung up on me. When I got there today, the traces were all cleaned up; I was surprised. When I went to inspect his room, everything looked fine but I knew to look for what the eyes do not see, so I proceeded to remove the posters on the walls and doors. Unsurprisingly, I found a hole on the fire door. He probably punched it in a rage: With his head.

I had been told Lloyd's girlfriend had been living in the house for over ten days. I confronted her and asked her how long she had been here, she answered four, and I told her she had to leave. I quoted the law also. I proceeded to leave a rule note for all tenants and I posted one in the corridor.

Here is the note:

Notice to all tenants at DOW14

According to the Housing of Multiple Occupancy regulations, it is illegal to have more than five unrelated adults dwelling in this property. This means that no more than five people may overnight at this address from now on. Anybody who refuses to comply will see his or her tenancy agreement terminated with immediate effect.

Due to the extreme wear and tear and damages to the property, it is now prohibited to receive any friends or family members into the house during inappropriate hours without my prior knowledge and consent. Inappropriate hours, by definition, mean hours when other tenants are sleeping or simply enjoying the comforts of their homes, i.e. evenings and weekends. Only contracted tenants are allowed to stay in the property.

It is your duty to report to me if the rules are broken by your fellow tenants.

A more frequent inspection of the house will now take place until further notice. Photographic evidence of damages will be taken at each inspection as evidence.

Any tenant who refuses to cooperate will be notified by us in writing and will be reported to the authorities, i.e. the police, and will have their names forwarded to all local and national landlord's associations and estate agencies.

If you disagree with these new rules, you are free to terminate your tenancy agreement and leave. A week's notice would do. If no damages have been done to your room and to the house, you will be fully refunded your deposit within ten working days.

When I got home, I wrote a letter to Lloyd, enclosing pictures of the damaged door, which will be hand-delivered the following day. I also sent him and his father a copy in an email. I called his father to explain the situation too. He quite understood, and he asked me if I had forwarded it to his wife, Selina; I responded that I did not have her email. He would forward it to her. Here is the letter:

Subject: Damaged Door

Date: 15 March 2011

Dear Mr Lawson,

After the inspection of your room at DOW14 this morning, we have found damage done to the door despite your attempt to cover it with a poster.

The cost to replace the door is in the range of £500 with labour and VAT. An exact cost will be assessed by us and the total cost transferred to you. If you wish to replace it yourself, we will gladly allow you to do so, subject to it being professionally done and having a twelve-month guarantee.

We expect the door to be repaired within ten working days starting from today.

A photograph of the damage is hereby attached.

According to the law, the house cannot have more than five unrelated adults in this property, which means that your girlfriend has to leave the property immediately. I understand she has been residing in the property for more than ten days.

In addition to the above breach of contract, please remember that the house is a home for the other tenants. Hence, your friends are kindly invited to find another gathering spot outside the premises.

Should you refuse to comply with terms of your contract, you will be removed from the property.

In order to keep the peace in the house, frequent inspections will be done until further notice.

I expect you to do the right thing.

Regards

Taiwo Orishayomi

I am now in the process of evicting him. I will be seeking the advice of people who have been through this kind of situation. I decided to liaise with my local council; specifically, the private tenancy team.

16 March 2011

Wow, what a brilliant day! First, I showed my last room today to an Italian guy who came down to Bristol for twenty-four hours just to find a suitable room. I had forgotten about the appointment; luckily, I was heading for the house to sign the AST with the couple who took my double room yesterday. Lorenzo saw the room, and I told him that the area was very much in demand and he had to make up his mind as soon as possible. I told him that rooms at the BOS1 property had become available just three days ago and that three out of the four rooms were already gone. He was quite impressed by the standard of the house. Off he went to view more rooms. About an hour later, he called to tell me he wanted the room. I told him I could meet him at the house a couple of hours later. I did that and took a £380 deposit from him. It is now my rule to take a full month's deposit instead of just £50 as I used to, simply because it is more difficult for them to lose a full month's deposit rather than £50. I was let down a couple of times.

I met Geoff Whittaker today for the training. Geoff and I had crewed quite a few times for the Duo. We always share strategies and ideas. During the last property super conference, I told him about my strategy; he immediately booked a one-to-one meeting. I spent half of the day doing the theory side of my strategy and real life examples. I took Geoff to view three of my HMOs; he saw me sign the AST with Lorenzo and serve Lloyd Lawson with the legal letter.

All the rooms at the BOS1 property were now fully rented. I can probably get another house this month.

A couple contacted me on Easyroommate regarding my large double room in Fishponds. I called them and arranged a viewing of the room for Friday. I might get that rented by the end of the week.

17 March 2011

Thank God, Manu did not commit suicide or anything, he just ran away leaving his room in a mess, with dirty plates, pots, and pans everywhere. He had now lost his deposit. The room would be rented out within a few days as I have a waiting list for double rooms.

I understood that Manu was incapable of living with other people. He fought with everyone in the house and he complained about everything. He was the one who called me for help when the wind outside was getting too loud. He also called me for help because he could not stand the smell of fresh linen. Manu was a coward who was incapable of defending himself. He was a real Joker

I went to plaster all the cracks in one of my large double rooms in Fishponds; tomorrow, I will put on a coat of paint to freshen up the room. I have three people coming tomorrow to view it. I intend to get that out of the way by the end of next week.

I went to measure Lloyd's door to give the measurement to his parents. The measurements are as follows:

Height: 6 feet 3 inches

Width: 2 feet 4 inches

Thickness: 1¾ inches

I spoke with the tenants at DOW14 regarding Lloyd; it is now their choice if they want him to stay or leave. His tenancy runs out in six weeks' time.

18 March 2011

My day started at 6.30 a.m. today. I had to get to the NEW61 property to freshen up the walls. Yesterday, I filled all the cracks on the walls. I had to get everything ready before 11 a.m. for my first viewing.

After sanding down the filler, I put a coat of magnolia paint on the retouched part, then I realised that the magnolia I bought was slightly darker than the one that was used previously. I had to paint the whole room, which I did within two hours. I now consider myself as one of the fastest painters in the land.

The room was freshened up and I was ready for my viewing. The couple arrived on time; they just fell in love with the room. They took it immediately; they paid the deposit and the first month's rent straightaway. I had my second appointment arrive as I was signing the contract. Greg was disappointed because the room was gone, as it was exactly what he was looking for. Luckily, I had Manu's former room just round the corner, but it was not yet ready for viewing. I decided to show him anyway, but I did not think he would take it.

My cleaner came to clean the room, and so made it ready for my third viewing. Alan came but was not impressed; I was not impressed by him either.

I popped in to KIM40 for a quick inspection; everything looked good. My day ended by 3 p.m. I got home, opened my pile of letters, organised them according to properties, and filed them. It is good to have all bills set up on direct debit; it just makes everything easier.

I also took pictures of Manu's room; they might be needed in the future. The pictures were taken before my cleaner did her magic work. It is a must for any HMO landlord to always carry a camera. You need to be able to take pictures of, or even film, any event that might get out of hand.

I have to wake up very early tomorrow to head for my five-day training with the HMO daddy!

19 March 2011

What a day! I woke up this morning at 5.30 a.m. and set off on the road at 6:30 a.m. I got to Wednesbury at 8.45 a.m. The course started at 10 a.m.

There were seven of us training with the Daddy, Jim. Jim has a two-storey office cabin at the back of one of his houses. He uses downstairs as his office and upstairs as the training or meeting room.

We all gathered there after some small talk and introductions to one another. Frank Wolley, my fellow investor whom I had known for a year, was also there. I paid for my seat but he had won his!

Jim started by handing us all his manual of over 300 pages of everything he knows about HMOs.

That manual alone is worth gold. A few hours into the training, I realised that everything I had been doing for the past four months was, in fact, okay. Although I wasn't sure if I was doing the right thing legally, Jim confirmed that I was on the right track. I threw in some questions I had previously prepared.

We took a tea break at about 11 a.m. and then went back to the training room. We were there until about 1.30 p.m. We then went out for lunch. Immediately after lunch, we went on a tour of Jim's houses, which was the most exciting part of the day. Jim has given a new definition to space management.

Jim's tenant demographic had moved from just 6 per cent to 60 per cent LHA tenants since the beginning of the economic downturn. So, the people we saw taking the rooms were mostly smokers and they smoked in the rooms. I asked Jim why he allowed them to smoke in the rooms; he said that there was no way of enforcing the smoking ban when 90 per cent of the tenants smoked.

Most of Jim's rooms are self-contained, which means that there is usually a kitchenette with a fridge, freezer, microwave, and kettle. And there is a shower box room with a small shower and toilet. So the rooms are more like mini studios. There is usually a communal kitchen downstairs for those who wish to cook; he says that very few people cook. This is the complete opposite of my tenants. Most of them are from France, Italy, and Spain. They always cook.

Because most of his tenants are now LHA, and because LHA does not pay more than £60 per week for a simple room and £90 for a studio, Jim will creatively manage the space to make it a £60-a-week room or a £90-a-week room, no matter how big or small the room is. Jim will split large rooms into two self-contained rooms. So where he would initially only get £90 per week, he now gets double the money: genius!

We went from house to house, from new conversions to older ones. Jim builds small chalets in the gardens of some of his houses and uses them as extra space: again, genius!

It was a good insight into the other side of the HMO market. It is a demography I would not want to deal with. I will like to keep my HMOs strictly for professionals, although I could have an LHA tenant per house if necessary.

One of the questions I asked Jim was, if he were to start again, would he buy so many houses. He said he probably would stop at about fifty properties. Beyond that figure, one has to have staff; controlling staff and getting them to work is a whole new issue.

Jim no longer buys, but he now does lease options with tired landlords who just hand him their keys. I told him about my strategy of taking company lets from letting agencies and letting to professionals. He was pretty amazed by my success. I call my strategy Rent2Rent.

After the tour, we went back to the office to finish the theory part of the training, which ended at 6.30 p.m. We all went downstairs where we had a glass of wine before heading for the restaurant.

Some of us would be attending the eviction course the following day. Jim kindly put us all up in his empty studios, saving us all money.

I went to bed pretty exhausted! Tomorrow is another day.

20 March 2011

Today was the DIY eviction day with Jim. The course was from 10 a.m. until 4 p.m., with a break for lunch in the middle.

Jim gave us all a second manual with legal forms and case studies. It was very important to know what to do in case of bad tenants. The key point of the course was to avoid getting that far; instead, Jim advised us to keep the communication going right from the start. Never lose one's temper and do not get emotional about the tenant's situation either. Suggest different ways of finding a solution and if worse comes to worst, ask them when they intend to leave. Always sign a waiver form when they give the keys back. The form will always prevent them from trying to sue you in the future.

It is quite frustrating to see that the whole system is geared to destroy landlords. Jim's step-by-step knowledge is such a valuable tool for any landlord.

I was thinking of staying a further three days on the training ground, but I knew quite a lot already and that part was more suitable for complete beginners. Jim praised me for my achievements in such a short period, a great compliment from such a man. I would recommend Jim's courses to anyone who wishes to go into the HMO business.

I left at 4.30 p.m. and drove back to Bristol. The journey took about an hour and half. When I got home, I went through my emails and the marketing I had not been able do for the past two days.

A weekend well worth it! Jim is really the expert in this field and I was glad I took his course.

21 March 2011

A day of rest.

22 March 2011

I started the day by inspecting all my houses, collecting all mails, and checking that the houses were well cleaned. I received a call from Ainsley and his girlfriend about a leak at the NEW61 property. I informed GM, the agent, and a plumber was sent immediately.

After a few hours, they called me again to inform me that the door of the washing machine was broken.

I received an email from Pablo, the Spanish guy who moved in the month before, telling me that he needed to move in a month and he wanted to use his deposit as his last month's rent. Experience had taught me that when people want to use their deposit money as their last month's rent, it usually means that they no longer have a job. I told him he was not only breaching his contract but also that there was no way he could possibly use his deposit as rent. I tried to see him several times today but he was never there.

I had three appointments today for the LOD47 property; nobody seems to be very interested.

I went to see an old woman who was selling her b. & b., wanting to book an appointment with her. She agreed to show me the house the following day at 1 p.m. I planned to go there with Frank. She also told me that the previous prospective buyer had not sent in a surveyor yet, which meant that we had a greater chance of getting the place.

I asked Frank to start speaking with his "cash-rich contact", as we were planning to buy the house in cash, renovate it, and then mortgage it.

The couple at DOW14 called me this evening about a series of insect bites they both have all over their bodies. I went to see them after my viewings at 7.30 p.m. and they surely had a lot of bite marks. I took some pictures, which I intend to show to a specialist tomorrow. They also picked up a dead insect and put it in a jar for me to take away. In my opinion, they are exaggerating the situation and I think that they simply let in some mosquitoes. Another answer would be perhaps their desire to leave the house. Who knows? According to my knowledge, when someone starts to look for and find problems, that often means that they want to leave and they need a viable reason to break the contract.

Esteban, my Spanish tenant at BOS1 Road, texted me again, telling me that the boiler had stopped producing hot water. I asked him to press the reset button. He texted back that it now works. Good Lord!

There is a house just opposite NEW61 that has been empty for over six months. I finally decided to ask the neighbours about it. I went around and I found a woman who was nice enough to give me some information. The woman had been living there for over thirty years, and she said that the owner "had more money than sense". She said that the house belonged to the mother of the owner, and that he had been doing some renovations before the crisis hit the country. He had had to pull out the builders, and the house had been empty for the past eighteen months or so.

I would try to find out more about it. I hope I would strike a deal with the owner.

Tomorrow would be a better day, with only good news!

23 March 2011

Bed Bugs

I called a pest control company after researching bed bugs on the Internet. The photos I took of my tenants yesterday match the pictures of other people bitten by bed bugs.

I spoke with a company called Pest Force, also with Andy and Iain, who explained the issue to me. It seems that many developed countries are been infected by these insects, including very clean places. Pest Force quoted £180 for three treatments. I gave him the go-ahead.

Frank, Amily, and I went to the b. & b. for our first viewing. The house is huge and we could fit in at least thirteen good-sized rooms. We estimate the refurbishment would be in the range of £40K. Frank will speak with his cash-rich contact tonight and we would be able to put in an offer by the end of the week.

I had a viewing today at LOD47; the woman came quickly but did not seem impressed either. A single room will also be available as of tomorrow in the same house.

I viewed three properties today with Olivia, the GM Bristol representative. The Balaclava Road house was of no interest to me due to its location, but the two in Boston Road were. As I already had three on that street, I might as well extend them to five. The area is very good; it is close to Gloucester Rd and the hospital. One of the houses seemed empty; I expressed my interest in it. I might be able to get that one by this time next week.

Tomorrow, I should be meeting Kumar regarding his house in Whitchurch. I had few requests for that area.

24 March 2011

My day started pretty easily today. As time has gone by, and as I approach my ten-property figure, I have been enjoying my job a lot more. I have thirty units; two rooms recently available.

I dropped all the electricity and gas bills at all the houses for the tenants to see. I then drove to check if the fire extinguishers ordered for the BOS9 property had arrived. There, one of the tenants asked if I could find two rooms for his friends who would be arriving soon in Bristol. Yes, I said.

I met Kumar and Graham regarding his house in Whitchurch. Graham had prepared a plan for a new kitchen fitted with all appliances, new wiring, and full window replacement. The cost was around £12K for the essentials and a further 5K for redecorating.

It would be a good experience if we got the job.

I spoke with John, one of my LHA tenants, about his rent delay, I asked for his caseworker at the council and I called to verify his story. He was indeed telling the truth. The council told me I should receive my money within the next five working days.

I also got around to writing official letters to Joe, who needed a weekly reminder of his rent payment, and Lee, who still owes the deposit.

The letters go as follows:

Date: 24 March 2011

Dear Lee,

As of today, we only have received £20 towards your deposit of £355. You still owe us £335, which must be paid entirely in the next ten days.

I believe you now work full time and there should not be any issue about making the payment. Please bear in mind that non-payment will result in your eviction from the property.

Should you not agree and wish to make further arrangements, feel free to contact me.

Regards

Taiwo Orishayomi

24 March 2011

Dear Joe,

Due to the lack of communication and lack of your rent payment, I am hereby giving you a warning.

Since the day that you moved into the property, you have required multiple reminders and phone calls in order to make your rent payments. *You still owe £200 towards this month's rent plus £55 penalty charges accumulated from the 13th.*

You are required to make the payment in the next five days. Failure to do so will see you evicted from the property for good.

Should you need to make other arrangements in order to make the payments, feel free to contact me as soon as possible.

Regards

Taiwo Orishayomi

Late payers get no rest as far as I'm concerned.

25 March 2011

I met with Geoff today; long day talking about our JV potential.

26 March 2011

I spent the day post carding in Fishponds. I had printed out an advertisement and had gone around shops to put them on windows. Some were free and some shop owners asked for payments between 50p and £1.

Single and Double Rooms available in this area.

No agency fee!

Couples welcome!

Professional houses, no pets or children.

Rooms are from £300 pcm, most bills inclusive.

Wireless Internet

Fully furnished

Free parking

Garden

Washing machine/dryer

Dishwasher

Separate lounge

Council Tax, water, TV licence, weekly cleaner all inclusive in the rent.

Close to bus routes

Clean, tidy houses

To arrange a viewing for one of our rooms, call Lauren on 07727671675

27 March 2011

I usually do not like working on Sundays, but sometimes, if a room is empty, I will make the effort to do a viewing. This Sunday, a couple came, but I did not think they would go for it. I was now wondering if I shouldn't repair the entrance of the LOD47 property, as the paint on the side of the house is off. GM refuses to repair it. I had a quote of £100 to do the job. I went for the quote.

28 March 2011

The council came to view the room that would become available in a couple of days. Due to the quantity of rooms that would be empty at the end of April, I had decided to approach the council and rent a couple of single rooms to them. My appointment with them was this morning at 11 a.m. and the tenant, Daniel, forgot to change his clock, so he did not turn up.

The room was £355 pcm, but I would leave it to the council for £330 pcm.

This evening, one of the tenants at the DOW14 house called to give me his notice. I advertised it immediately. It is in a good area and should go in a few days.

The tenant who forgot to show up this morning has just called to rearrange his viewing for tomorrow at 2 p.m.

29 March 2011

For the first time in months, I decided to start my day very late, by that I mean 2 p.m.

I met with Daniel at NEW61. He was there on time and well presented. Daniel was twenty seven and worked at Bristol Zoo as a photographer. The council would pay half of his rent, and he would pay the rest. We had a long chat, and he seemed to be worthy of a chance.

I received a call from a man this afternoon asking for a double room as soon as possible. I asked if he could pay. He said he was starting a job in a week and would be able to do so then. I told him I had heard everything before and if he could not come up with a month's rent and a month's deposit, he could keep looking elsewhere. I think he had seen one of my advertisements in a shop. And he called me "Love"! Do not get me started on that one.

Back to Daniel, I have arranged for him to move in tomorrow, Gilbert, the former tenant moves out tonight.

I received an email form Lorenzo, the Italian man who took one of my doubles at BOS1. He will be arriving later to Bristol as planned, so he offered to pay for the month, just for me to keep the room for him. I sent him my bank details for the transfer.

I received my limited company statement today, and I hit the £10,000 gross income mark, not bad for a business that started only four months ago! When I get to ten properties, I will take a couple of months' break.

I spent some hours posting ads and updating them. Many emails were received from people looking for accommodation at the end of April.

30 March 2011

Joe called me at almost 11 p.m. last night to tell me that the keys to his door had jammed. I asked if he had been having problems previously, and he said he had. But also, he had always managed to open the door. I said he should have let me know right from the start. I told him to oil the key and keep trying. Joe has been a late payer right from the beginning. He has been avoiding my calls for weeks and is late again in paying his rent. This morning, I received a text he had sent at midnight asking me to send a locksmith.

I called Andrews, the LA whom I took the house from, and a locksmith was sent this morning. I went to see the door and they explained that Joe had broken his key inside the lock, which had caused the door to jam completely. The problem was solved there and then.

I received a call from Mihai this morning regarding the double room his friend wanted. He had previously asked me if I would have something available for the end of the month. Good timing, Manu's old room was still available. I took them both for a viewing and she took it. We would be signing the contract this Friday for LOD47.

Gilbert's room at NEW61 became vacant last night, Daniel moved in today. James from the council came along to arrange the contracts.

My two appointments at 4 and 6 p.m. were both cancelled just few minutes before they were due to arrive! Early finish today, then!

31 March 2011

End of the month

In order to systematise my strategy, I decided to collect the meter readings at the end of each month. I spoke with the energy company who have now set me up as a landlord. All I need to do at the end of each month is to send them a table of all my properties and meter readings.

My first month goes as follows:

Property	Date	Electricity	Gas
KIM40	30/03/2011	18816	4170
LOD47	30/03/2011	58248	8316
NEW61	30/03/2011	49375	09858
BRE37	30/03/2011	02935	03275
DOW14	30/03/2011	60083	9794
BOS9	30/03/2011	N/A	11550
BOS1	30/03/2011	79877	1148

Also, as part of my contribution, I have set up a £50 monthly donation to House of Mercy children's rescue, a charity started in 2006 by a friend of mine. I will add the charity to my www.bristol-rentals.com website.

The b. & b. JV I was considering doing with Frank Wolley looked shaky, as he had now come back to me saying that the investor he had in mind wanted to do one thing at a time. To me, the excuse was probably something else. I therefore emailed all the potential JVs I know. If nothing comes through, I will consider selling the deal.

It was a nice and quiet day today. April fool!

2 April 2011

Today I showed DOW14 to the first potential tenant. She was looking to move towards the end of April, which was a perfect time. Then I noticed that all the trees in the garden had been cut down and a bonfire set in the middle of the garden. I asked Maciej, one of the tenants who did the cleaning of the garden, and he said it was John, the LHA tenant I had been helping.

I immediately called John, who told me he was trying to help clean the garden. I asked him if he had read his tenancy agreement, stating that no modifications were to be done to the property without my consent. He apologised as usual, but I was furious.

One of the letting agents I rented the place from was coming to inspect the house on Tuesday 5 April, and the place needed to be spotless. So I asked John to remove all of the twigs from the garden. He promised to find a car and get rid of them. But to make sure, I intended to pop by tomorrow, Sunday. I would drop off Lloyd Lawson's eviction letter too.

After long conversations with the DOW14 tenants and after one couple decided to give me their notice to leave because of Lloyd Lawson's behaviour, I had decided to evict him. According to the law and his contract, I had to give four weeks' notice. The eviction letter went like this:

Subject: Letter of non-renewal of contract

Date: 2 March 2011

Tenant: Lloyd Lawson

Dear Mr Lawson,

I hereby inform you that STAK Property Investors Ltd will not be renewing your tenancy after 3 April 2011.

Due to many negative incidents during your stay at DOW14, we feel that you will be more suitable in a student accommodation rather than in a mature, professional one.

We therefore give you four weeks' notice as per the contract, starting from 3 April 2011. You may terminate your contract earlier if you find a suitable accommodation but you must vacate your room by 3 May 2011.

Please make sure that the door that you have broken is replaced and no further damage is done to the above-mentioned property during the remaining weeks.

Your deposit will be refunded after inspection of your room and deduction of the energy used during your stay.

I will be happy to write you a good reference in the future if you ever need it.

I wish you all the best.

Taiwo Orishayomi

STAK Property Investors Ltd.

This would be my very first eviction. Let's see how that goes.

8 April 2011

After a few days off, the workload I faced was quite heavy: Several bills to deal with, a lot of payments to deal with, and of course many tenants' requests to deal with.

The BOS71 property was now mine. It would be available only from early June; which meant that I would have two properties to fill that month. The total number of my houses was now nine.

I decided not to get any more properties that month. I would get one in May, which would make it ten.

Lloyd seemed to be taking his eviction well. He was now looking for another place. I offered a room in Fishponds but he did not seem to want it.

The good weather was bringing out the sunshine in most of my tenants. Some decided to clean up the garden, while some decided to rebuild the garden. Of course, some expected me to buy them garden furniture too, seriously!

The second and last bug treatment at DOW14 property took place yesterday, so there should be no further bug issues. The bugs came from the second-hand bed I had bought. The bug man said that there were probably just two bugs and that I did the right thing by calling him early. These bugs reproduce fast in the right environment. Lesson learned, always buy new beds. The cost was just £90.

Frank and I are still working on the b. & b.; he found an investor who seems interested. If he goes ahead and invest, he would fund 100 per cent, but with some securities.

I am also working on my one-day course material. As soon as I reach ten properties, I will start promoting it.

LOD47 entrance is now fully renovated at my expense. I asked Graham to paint the bare bricks that were making the house look old. The job cost me £100. I like my houses to be clean and tidy, inside out.

11 April 2011

I spent the day with Geoff Whittaker, the man I was mentoring. We spent the day going through our plan for the next couple of days. We also took time to reflect on a potential future collaboration in coaching my Rent2Rent strategy.

12 April 2011

As part of Geoff's training, I decided to do some viewings with him in first few weeks. We started the day by viewing a house in Bishopston; oddly, the viewing was with an agent I had used in the past. The house was not in a good location. It was too far towards the centre and above a shop. Very few buses, just two, go near the centre. The layout was also a problem: only one room had access to the garden. The kitchen was upstairs with no windows. I wondered what the architect was thinking. Our second viewing was cancelled because the agent's car broke down. Our fourth viewing was also cancelled because we went to the wrong address, and our fifth one was in a very good location but the house was a shambles.

We spent the whole day just driving from one place to another; we got stuck in the traffic. Hopefully tomorrow will be better.

13 April 2011

I spent the day with Geoff on viewings; three properties stood out. One is a four-bedroom in Filton, opposite Airbus. The location was great but the state of the house was awful. The second one stood out: a seven-bedroom, four-storey house in Montpellier, at walking distance to the city centre. Great location, beautiful newly refurbished house, but the only issue was that it had no HMO licence.

The third one was a four-bedroom house in Fishponds, also great location but it had an infestation of wood lice. The floor of the sitting room was covered in dead wood lice.

I told Geoff to put offers on both the Fishponds and the Montpellier houses.

The Montpellier asking price was £1800 pcm and Fishponds was £925. His profit would be around £900 pcm for the first and £527 for the latter, according to my calculations.

14 April 2011

Geoff called me to raise questions that were bugging him. I told him not to look at the problems but to focus on the positive stuff. Anyway, to cut a long story short, he decided not to go for the Montpellier house. He asked me if I wanted it. I took it straight away.

I also decided to take a second look at the one near Airbus. Surprisingly, the landlord had taken care of the clutter and cleaned the place, and he was also willing to update the house. So I decided to take that as well. The profit was not great but there was potential in there.

I also saw a four-bedroom house with GM in Filton, also close to Airbus. I had put in my offer. If it is accepted, I will move into that one in July, giving me time to sort out my finances.

All in all, I had twelve properties, fifty-five units, £6,627 pcm profit; not bad for a business started just five months ago.

I decided to take a break late July.

17 April 2011

Today I had a viewing with a polish couple for the double room at DOW14. They saw it and liked it but are still hesitant. Luckily, my other Polish tenant came down and spoke with them in Polish, I couldn't understand the conversation; all I knew was that they took the room straightaway, and even recommended a friend for the single room upstairs. That was Lloyd's room which would be vacant from 3 May.

18 April 2011

I had a meeting with my accountant. He will be submitting a cash flow record on a monthly basis from now on. I submitted all my paper work for the Norrisville and Filton Avenue houses.

I have started advertising all the rooms and a lot of interest is being generated for the Norrisville house. I think it would go within a day or so. These are the houses that Geoff decided not to take, the Montpellier house and the one in near Airbus.

19 April 2011

I had a viewing this evening with Kevin; he saw BRE37 and KIM40. He went for the large double room in KIM40. We signed the contract there and then. He will be transferring the month deposit.

I asked my bank for an overdraft facility yesterday, which they automatically turned down due to my early stage of the account. I explained that I would move all my personal and business accounts if they do not reconsider their decision. For almost four months, my business account has been doing very well and turning over £10K per month. I did not need the facility, but my accountant advised me to get one just in case. It is also good for my bank records.

They came back to me with a forecast request, which I will spend time doing this evening.

20 April 2011

The first thing I did this morning was to go visit Zed and Co estate agent, the agent managing the Norrisville house. I got there about 9.30 a.m. but the office was closed. I was there until past 10 a.m. I asked the neighbouring shops if there was any information they could give me regarding their opening times; none was able to help.

I spoke with Key Lettings, a competitor just a few doors away. They told me the shop was owned by a guy called Zed, and that there was nothing wrong according to them.

I came back to visit the shop around 2.30 p.m. The shop was still closed, but the neighbour told me they had been open earlier on. Still none of my calls, texts, or emails was returned. I started to worry about the genuine activity of this letting agency.

The house in Filton was going well, and I should have the keys as planned.

21 April 2011

I went to Zed and Co again this morning to see if the agency was open. They were; I quickly parked my car and ran to the shop just in case they closed before I got there. I saw Naila, the agent that never returns calls.

She told me that she had mentioned that my file would not be looked into before Thursday, something I was almost certain was not mentioned. I told her to get in touch with me if she needed any information. That evening at about 4.30 p.m., I received a call from them asking me to pop into the office as soon as possible, I told them I had plans already but could see them on Friday morning.

22 April 2011

I went to the office to see Zed, the owner of the agency. He is an Indian man. He asked me for all sorts of paperwork. I asked him if this was personal because none of the agencies I use has ever asked for my bank statements, a guarantor, a letter from my accountant, and letters from all other agencies I have used in the past. Zed also said that despite all the paperwork requested there was no guarantee I would get the house. Now that was new!

The lesson I learnt was to stay away from small agencies. They tend to judge by the cover.

Here by is the copy of letter sent to him:

Dear Zed,

Just to recapitulate our meeting this morning. You have requested the below documentation from me:

- A certified six-month account from my accountant
- A reference on letterhead from GM, with whom I have seven properties.
- A reference on letterhead from Andrews letting agents, with whom I have two properties.
- A reference on letterhead from CJ Hole, with whom I am in the process of taking a property.

- Six months of bank statements
- A guarantor letter

Please bear in mind that CJ Hole is a new agency and we are in the process of completing our first project; however, I will provide you the name and contact details of the person in charge of my account. Feel free to contact them.

I have not been given any guarantor form from your agency; please let me know what exactly you would need from my guarantor.

I am yet to receive the acknowledgement of the transfer of the £756 agency fee made on Monday, 18 April. An email receipt would do.

If after all the above requirements you still doubt my ability to make the payments, I would need my £756 back promptly along with all the confidential documents submitted.

I hope to develop a long lasting work relationship with your agency, as I have with the above-mentioned agencies since I started my business a few months ago.

Kind Regards

25 April 2011

I drove back directly to KIM40 from my short weekend away. The former tenants had cleaned the rooms but not properly, and my new tenants were due to arrive just in an hour. I had all my gloves and cleaning gear in the boot of my car, so I scrubbed for the next forty minutes.

That is part of the sacrifice. One has to get down and dirty when needed. I cleaned houses once to pay for my studies. I will do it again if I have to.

26 April 2011

I spent the day getting together all the documentations for Zed and Co. I got the references from GM, Andrews, and CJ Hole, gathered all account details, and also got my payment confirmation. It seems that Zed was finally waking up to the professional world.

I went to all my houses to collect the meter readings and letters. The BOS1 property needed the garden to be cleared, so I called John Goatley, the LHA tenant who owes some money. I had told him I would call him for odd gardening jobs to pay off what he owes. I have therefore arranged to pick him up on Thursday to work on the BOS1 property garden. If a tenant cannot pay, why not accept work in lieu of the money owed?

I finally got around to doing some administrative work, so I registered some properties on the Council Tax website to make online payments.

The house near Airbus in Filton was confirmed; I would sign the contract on 3 May.

28 April 2011

I received a call from Zed today informing me that he had decided not to give me the Norrisville house. His decision was based on the fact that my guarantor did not earn enough. I know that his decision was only racially based. I asked for my deposit back in full but he refused to answer.

If the worse comes to worst, I will sue him.

John Goatley, one of the DOW14 property tenants, was doing a bit of gardening at BOS1 in lieu of two weeks' rent he owed me. He had spent seven hours at it, he said. I will go and check his work.

2 May 2011

Today I took the keys back from Lloyd. Both his parents were there; his dad had painted the new door and his mum had dealt with the papers. Before heading to the meeting, I wrote a waiver form, which states his and my responsibilities and most importantly, makes clear the impossibility of a legal action against me. An idea I got from Jim Haliburton. The form goes like this:

Waiver form

Date: 2 May 2011

I hereby agree to vacate my room after having been given four weeks' notice.

A similar room was suggested by Taiwo Orishayomi in Fishponds, which, I, Mr L. Lawson, chose not to accept.

I hereby consent to:

- Leave the room in the same condition as it was at the beginning of the tenancy.
- Repair the broken door.
- Leave all copies of keys to the house.
- Pay my share of utilities used during my stay in the house (DOW14).

I, Taiwo Orishayomi, STAK PI Ltd, consent to refund Mr Lawson his deposit after the deduction of his share of the energy used in the house during the period of ninety days. Refund will be made within the following twenty days.

Refund will be made to Mr Lawson's account as stated below:

Bank:

Sort code:

Account Number:

No legal action would be taken by either party as long as the above conditions are met.

Signature: Taiwo Orishayomi

Signature: Mr Lloyd Lawson

After the meeting, I went straight to KIM40 property to show a couple one of the double rooms.

The wife was four months pregnant, and they wanted the room for five months. I agreed to let them the house until the baby was born.

As soon as they entered the house, they liked it and took the double room. We signed the contract there. They would move in on Wednesday.

I have two more rooms to rent at KIM40. My intention was to have everything let out by the end of that week. I had two viewings the following day with another couple.

3 May 2011

Today I started at 6.30 a.m. and finished at 10 p.m. Many events took place and I spent the day running from one appointment to another.

First, I picked up John from DOW14 to finish the gardening work at the BOS1 property. After that, I ran up to BRE37 for boiler repairs, again. Then I ran to my appointment with Zed and Co regarding my upfront fee for Norrisville. I stayed and argued with them for forty minutes in the attempt to get my entire £756 fee back. Naila, the woman who showed the house in the first place, decided to return just 50 per cent of my money, to which I laughed. They gave several reasons for refusing me the property, reasons, of course, that could not stand up in a court. To cut a long story short, I took 75 per cent of my fee in a cheque and I told them that the rest would be decided in court.

Secondly, I went to finalize the tenancy agreement for the FIL949 property. I paid almost £1,800 by card, took the keys and all paperwork, and went to the house for the inventory.

The house is fairly old and it shows that either the landlords do not have much money or they are simply very negligent. Some of the works I requested have been done, i.e. an additional bed was put in one of the rooms and new curtains installed in the house. But some have not been done, i.e. broken furniture and doors were not replaced. Some problems I noticed during the inventory, e.g. the bathroom lock is faulty.

My belief was that I should have negotiated the price even lower, to £650 or £700 at most. My £750 was way too much. Lesson learned.

Thirdly, I had three viewings for the KIM40 rooms; one cancelled and two others showed up. One Indian man wanted a house with just couples, and I had one, KIM40. He was an insecure lad and did not want his wife to be around other men. The other viewing was a guy looking for a long term contract; he was planning for his wife to join him in August.

Fourthly, I went to meet Jakub and his girlfriend the couple that took one of the double rooms at KIM40, for their payment. When I got there, I found they were only able to withdraw £200 from the cash machine. To avoid troubles for all, I decided to give them the contract and the keys to the house, and allow them to make the rest of the payment the following day.

Then as I was about to head back home at 7 p.m., I received a call from David, who had been thrown out by his wife the day before and who urgently needed a room. So I took him to the KIM40 property to look at the smallest double, which was on the market for £365. He loved the room but wanted me to drop the price. I said no way. I told him to have a think and call me back the following day.

Fifthly, when I got home, I received a call from Frank, with whom I had been conversing all day regarding the b. & b. We decided to put in an offer today. He asked me what offer I had in mind and I replied that our final price should be £280K. We decided to start with £275K, leaving us some room to move up. He told me later that he had put in £270K; we settled at £272K: A fantastic deal and a fantastic way to end the day. Frank already has nine buy-to-let properties, so I trusted his expertise on negotiating the price.

4 May 2011

I woke up today with a key objective in mind, and that was to write a legal letter to Zed and Co. I called Homelet for their referencing price list. This is the agency that Zed and Co uses. To my surprise, it ranges from £14 to £30 per reference. After discovering this cost, there was no way I would allow Zed and Co to keep 25 per cent of my money as fee.

The letter went like this:

Final request for payment

To: Zed and Co

Subject: STAK PI LTD fee of £155

Date: 5 May 2011

Dear Sirs,

I am requesting finally in this letter the return of the balance of my application fee in respect to Norrisville Road, Bristol.

It is my belief that your decision to refuse to let the property to STAK PI Ltd is not due to STAK PI Ltd's incapability to pay the rent but to your own unfair assumptions.

To start, many mistakes were made by your agent, Naila, who had too much work to do during this period of time. I believe she was doing three people's work by her own acknowledgement, and by your own acknowledgement (Mr Zed), she had rented out a full months' stock in just eight days.

It was almost an impossible task to get a feedback from her either by phone, text, email, and even face-to-face. No calls were ever returned nor were emails replied.

The house was initially advertised for £1,700 pcm, and then at the viewing, it was boosted up to £1,800 pcm. Was this your first attempt to discourage us from putting in an offer?

When my student, Geoff Whittaker, first confirmed his interest in Norrisville Road, he immediately received a text requesting a payment of £756 to your account. Unfortunately, Geoff could not go further due to personal circumstances that arose that very day. I decided to take the property instead. Geoff's medical proofs can be supplied to support the circumstances.

When I texted Naila to inform her, she immediately replied, once again with a text, requesting the transfer of the money. The text was sent on 14 April 2011. I still have it saved on my phone.

However, I did not make the payment until the eighteenth because I needed further information. I came to the office on the eighteenth and I was asked if the transfer had been made, to which I replied no. Naila told me that in order to stop marketing the house I had to make the payment. At this point, I want to stress that *no paperwork was given nor was there any indication stressing your terms of payment.*

I was never informed, either verbally or in writing, that, should I fail the checks, I would not be refunded fully. I made the transfer on that very day and I was given a two-page application form to fill. I found it odd that the paperwork was so little. I asked if that was all and the answer was yes. Then I stressed that, should they need any further information, they could contact me by email or phone at any time.

I physically hand-delivered the application form the following day to Naila and heard nothing back for a whole week. I called and left messages on both your landlines and mobile, I even came to the office three times, just to find it closed. I spoke with the neighbours to ask if your office was out of business.

On my fourth attempt to meet face-to-face, I finally succeeded. Naila told me she had informed me that it would take a week to get back to me, information I am sure was not communicated. I know no other agency that takes a full week to get back to a potential business.

My question is, was this your second attempt to dissuade me from getting the house?

The only time I was given full information was when I had a meeting with Mr Zed on the 22/04/2011. He asked for the below documents:

A certified six-month account from my accountant

A reference on letterhead from Grant Management, with whom I have seven properties

A reference on letterhead from Andrews estate agents, with whom i have two properties

A reference on letterhead from CJ Hole, with whom I am in the process of taking a property

Six months of bank statements

A guarantor letter

Again, was this your third attempt to dissuade me from moving forward?

All of the above were presented on the 25/04/2011, except the certified six-month account, which, I explained to Naila, was not a possible task. My accountant's details were provided for further reference.

Despite all the above documents, you decided that I was not a suitable candidate, your reason being that my guarantor's salary was insufficient. Naila told me that my guarantor needed a salary of £61,000 per annum minimum, key information that came after the decision to refuse to let me the property had been made. For this reason, you made the assumption that my company was not capable of taking the house.

You also believe that you have done your best to secure the house for me.

My question to you now is, were your intentions to let me the property at all? I have reason to believe otherwise. I believe you already had a taker and I was just the backup plan, if anything at all.

First, I was not given an indication of how much you needed my guarantor to earn. Had you told me from the start that you needed a person who earns over 61,000 per annum, I would have simply asked my guarantor's husband to be added. Their household income is over £120,000 per annum. This household income can be verified either by calling their workplaces or simply by providing payslips for both guarantors.

Secondly, had you done your best to secure the property for me, you could have suggested I paid three months' rent upfront to see how it goes. And if after three months I had defaulted, you could have kicked me out. But in no way did you try to secure the property for me. I believe that, on the contrary, you have done your best to dissuade me from getting the property, the reasons being: a shameful lack of communication, extensive paperwork request, and the failure to research any of my references. None of the references was contacted at any point. GM, the agency with whom I have been collaborating for over six months and with whom I have seven properties, was never contacted. They could have confirmed to you that STAK PI LTD is by far their best client. Rent is always paid by direct debit on time and properties kept in impeccable state.

You claim to have spent £180 on my checks. I would like to see the receipt. In my opinion, a check does not cost more than £25 according to www.Landlord Referencing.co.uk. www. Homelet.co.uk referencing, which you have used, charges only £14 for a standard check and £30 for thorough check plus eviction letter. My belief is that you did not spend more than £24 on my checks. I see no justification for keeping £180. I will be happy to pay for one credit check only, a maximum of £25. You owe me £155 still.

According to the estate agency association: "There may be circumstances when you are not able to move into the property for reasons beyond your control, for example, your reference was not satisfactory or the agency has increased the rent. In these circumstances, it may be unfair for the agency not to return your holding deposit. If you have paid an administration fee and/or a holding deposit and the landlord chooses not to go ahead with the tenancy, the office of Fair Trading Guidance states that you should receive a refund of all pre-payments".

My interest is not to take you to court or to drag out this issue any further. It has wasted a lot of my time and yours. However, I will not hesitate to take the matter to court if I have to. I am not in the business of losing money. Every penny I spend is a penny I have worked hard for.

If you still refuse to refund my £155, I will not only request the £155 but also an amount for all expenses incurred in taking the matter to court and for my time spent in this matter.

I will report your conduct to the Ombudsman for Estate Agents, the National Association of Estate Agents, the Local Trading Standard Department, and all other estate agent related associations.

I believe that I have been treated unfairly and that too many assumptions were made by you without proof, and I ask that my money be returned by Tuesday 17 May. If I have not received this payment, I will be contacting my solicitor; a court action will result.

Please forward the payment to my bank account:

Bank

Sort: 00-00-00

Account: 00-00-00-00

Please send any response in writing to my office, 33 Victoria Street, BS1 6AS.

Regards

Taiwo Orishayomi

STAK PI Ltd

I sent the draft of the letter to both my business partners, Geoff and Frank; they checked it and gave me their feedback, which I applied. I sent the letter via recorded delivery, so the delivery could not be denied.

My new tenants, Jakub and Evelina, who just moved into KIM40, and whom I allowed to move in having paid just two weeks' rent, have still failed to pay me today as promised. Evelina is pregnant and Jakub has a job that pays just £6.50 hour: A very bad decision to have a baby in such a state.

I called him in the evening to enquire a bit more about his situation. I came to an arrangement with him to pay me weekly as long as he can provide his work details and the name and contact details of his boss. I will then call his boss to verify that he is working, and I will be the first to knock on his door when he gets paid, just as Jim Haliburton does with his difficult tenants. I know; I should have seen this coming. I was too nice and naïve, I guess.

5 May 2011

I wrote to my landlord and the letting agent from whom I took the FIL949 house. I explained to them that since I had been deceived, I would only agree for my contract to start when all works have been completed in the house. The letter goes like this:

> Dear Gina, Emily,
>
> I have to come back to you on this matter, as it was part of the requirements before I took over FIL949.
>
> I requested a PAT test to be done on all electrical appliances. This certificate is not among the paperwork given. While attempting to hoover the house yesterday, I noticed that the vacuum cleaners were broken or faulty, a condition that would have been picked up by the PAT engineer.
>
> Also, some of the repairs are yet to be done: Cupboard doors missing, broken dining table, etc.
>
> As it stands, I cannot move any of my executives into the house until all works are done. Had I known that these issues were still pending, I wouldn't have signed and paid. The agent who gave me the keys assured me that all works were done. This is misleading.
>
> Therefore, I request the tenancy to be put on hold and to be re-dated when all works are done.
>
> On another note, it was also my understanding that this was a property managed by CJ Hole; a solution much preferred.
>
> Kind regards

The landlord contacted me immediately to explain that due to the bank holidays, the works had been delayed and that she needed a few days to sort things out. I explained that I could not move in any of my executives in the state in which the house was currently. She asked me for the cooker measurement, which I provided. The PAT is my security to be able to let the house to the council if I have trouble letting it privately.

In the evening, I headed up to Taunton for Property Network West, which was a bit dry; just six people turned up. Bristol to Taunton is an hour drive, so I wasted two hours for nothing. A bit disappointed though.

6 May 2011

Today, I unexpectedly rented two rooms, one room in FIL949 and one in Fishponds, precisely BRE37. A former tenant of mine, Raymond, called me this morning asking if I had any rooms around LOD47 where he had lived for four months. I took him to see the large room in BRE37 and he took it.

I went to KIM40 to see Jakub and Evelina. Nice couple but very deceitful, so I cut a deal with them. They can pay me £350 for the room, paid weekly, but they have to handle the cleaning and tidying up of the garden and all communal areas. Since the girl does not work, she could do that. They were happy with the deal.

I was getting more and more calls, which meant that the high season was about to start. I have six rooms to fill before the end of this month.

7 May 2011

Today, Saturday, is also a working day for me. I had three viewings scheduled; two turned up. The first was a young man from Manchester. I showed him KIM40 and DOW14. He thought that KIM40 was too expensive and DOW14, which was within his budget, was too small.

My second viewing was with a woman from Westbury on Trym. She needed to move closer to her work. She was impressed but very indecisive. She called me after the viewings to confirm that she wanted to take a room at KIM40, then she called back to cancel. She wasted my time.

8 May 2011

I reserve Sundays for all administration work.

9 May 2011

The good thing about smartphones is that they make life easier but the bad thing is that when one does not have them for a day or two, one's work becomes a nightmare.

I have had my HTC phone for a couple of months and had to send it back for repair; it was faulty. My work this week is like going back to the dark ages. On advice, get a smartphone; it helps in building and mass texting your mailing list. One can also group tenants according to properties. If I want to deal with a particular house, I can mass text them with just a button.

This afternoon, I received a call from Mrs Irani, the landlady for FIL949, confirming all the works she was supposed to do before 3 May. A new cooker, a fridge, and a shower head had been installed. The old grout from the kitchen and bathroom had been removed. Locks had been installed on all doors and the PAT control had been done.

Joe Martin, the first tenant moved in last night, the cheeky fellow seized the opportunity to invite me for a bite, which I declined like a true lady. I don't mix business with pleasure. I received enquiries from many more people interested in the rooms and I was quite sure all the rooms would be let out by the end of this week. I also discovered that the house was close to Aztec West, a popular business compound.

I had a meeting today with the Wolleys, the family I am JVing with on the b. & b. We all met with Steve, the finance man, who explained the strategy to us. We are sending in a surveyor on Wednesday to give an evaluation of the house once all refurbishment has been completed. We are hoping for a final valuation of £550K at least.

Many viewings cancelled at the last minute lately due to my lack of due diligence. I have decided to fact-find before setting up any appointment from now on. My questions go like this:

- When do you need to move?

- Are you moving for work or internship?

- What is your budget?

- Are you looking for a double room or a single room?

- Is it just for you or for a couple?

- Will there be children or pets?

- How long are you planning to stay?

- What area specifically are you looking into?

If the answers were what I needed to hear, I would then set up a viewing.

Too many people have taken the addresses of the properties, but later called me back at the last minute to say that they were too far or too expensive, or that they had a cat, etc.

10 May 2011

Today Frank and I did the survey on the b. & b. Many solutions were put forward by the surveyor to achieve more with the house. We could potentially have a ten-bedroom HMO, two one-bedroom flats, and a plot of land for a detached house. We reckoned the potential value of the property would exceed £550K.

I popped in to the FIL949 property to check the works promised by the landlord. Locks have been put on all doors. The PAT test has been conducted, the rubbish has been taken out of the garden, and a new set of dining table and chairs put in. The house now looks presentable.

An appointment was cancelled with just thirty minutes' notice. A tenant from the NEW61 property gave me his notice today. The market had slowed down a bit; hopefully things would pick up soon.

13 May 2011

The only tenant at FIL949 was laid off today, so after just four days in the house, he gave me his notice. Today is definitely not my day!

14 May 2011

I rented out five rooms today. All the rooms at FIL949 were taken today, one room by a French Airbus engineer and the other three by three friends. Another room was taken at KIM40; I have just one room left there. Success, success!

16 May 2011

Today I started at 6.30 a.m. and I finished at 10 p.m. I moved the second tenant to FIL949; the demand for this house is much greater than I thought it would be. Many viewings have been booked for tomorrow. An Indian man called me late in the evening wishing to view the last double room in the house; he came, loved it, said that he works at Aztech West, and that the location was simply perfect. I told him to make a bank transfer, which will allow me to take his offer seriously, and hence remove the advertisement from the market. He called me an hour later to tell me that his Internet was not working and that he had made a phone transfer which would arrive on Wednesday. I told him that I needed a proof of transfer, which he could not give. Funny that when it comes to paying, computers and the Internet just mysteriously get bugged!

Joe, another tenant of mine from BOS9, who always pays late, texted me about leaving the house because I won't allow him to get a cat. I texted him back with my honest opinion, asking why a man who could barely pay his rent would want to take on additional burden by taking a cat. He did not like my comment, called me back immediately, argued with me, and then hung up. He claimed that I was angry because I did not want him to leave. Sure!

The good news of the day was the report of the survey for the b. & b. house. The surveyor valued the house at £385K, giving us a net discount of 41 per cent

After all work is done, the value will be in the region of £700K!

17 May 2011

The first thing I did this morning was to collect John and drive him to DOW14 to get him to pack his stuff and leave the house. I managed to get his case worker's number, called the Brooklyn Hall early intervention department, and spoke with Abbie, the caseworker. The team was very helpful and encouraged me to do whatever was necessary if I wished to kick him out. I was advised to follow the same procedure as anyone else. John is apparently not considered dangerous. My job now is to encourage him to leave as soon as possible.

The move cost me £30 in van hire; that is a high price for somebody I have already helped so much by giving a large discount. The lesson I learned here was not to allow rotten apples get into the basket. They are a waste of time, energy, and money. I had learned my lesson, or so I thought.

Joe, the liar at BOS9, texted to say he had paid; surprise, surprise, nothing arrived. His departure date was confirmed for 13 June. I could not wait to see the man leave.

Jazz, the Indian man who took the last double at FIL949, transferred his deposit last night at 11.30 p.m. The money came through straight away. Why the hell did he lie in the first place? Why would he say that he had made a telephone transfer when he did not? Many tenants lie the moment they open their mouths. Beware!

The best thing to do in this game is to have a set of *do*s and *don't*s and to stick to them. Many tenants lie as they breathe.

I called Zed and Co, the letting agency that wanted to keep part of my fee without giving me the house; well, I received their cheque today giving all my money back except the £25 I agreed to pay. Don't let anyone fool you. You get sharks everywhere.

25 May 2011

These days my tenants have been creating issues; perhaps this is part of the summer period, I cannot say. During winter, I heard nothing from them but the sunny days have been creating havoc.

Andrea Carter, one of my oldest tenants, asked if she could get a cat; my answer was no, being in a shared house. I told her that if she had the house for herself and her husband, a cat would be no issue, but as long as she was in a shared house, other tenants might not like the idea. To cut a long story short, we got into a serious argument.

Another tenant, Lee from BRE37, was like Joe from the BOS9 property. He never paid until I texted and called him. These guys just want me to fall sleep over their rent and forget about them. The case is totally the opposite; they tend to raise flags on my spreadsheet. I had told Lee that the company was under a new management and that he had to provide his NI number and a guarantor if he wishes to continue to live in the house. Hopefully, this will encourage him to leave.

Tim from LOD47 is another weird one. Tim's mother always pays and on time, but Tim hates changes. Tim is one of those men with anger issues, but his mother kept it well from me. I am now discovering the other side of the calm Tim. My first experience with this other side occurred when I put locks on his door as a security measure. Tim threatened to leave because of that. I answered that his wish to leave was not a problem for me and that he just needed to give me a months' notice. He texted back with an apology; that was three months ago.

LOD47 received an estimated winter bill last month, which they all paid. The total came to about £43 per head, not bad for a harsh winter. Then the accurate bill arrived this month, coming to about £47 per head. Again, not so bad when you think about it: £90 for gas and electricity during winter, for four months; anyway, Tim texted me angrily at 9.30 p.m., complaining about it.

I noticed that Tim acts on impulse without really thinking anything through. He did not look at the second page of the bill before telling me that I was asking for too much. I told him he needed to check the second page to find the electricity bill. Then he texted again telling me that he had already paid £90 last month towards the bill, I then reminded him that he had only paid £43. And it went on and on until I decided to give him a call to ask about his problems. An argument ensued; he hung up, and I gave him his months' notice to leave. He texted back that he would sue me; I told him to go ahead. I plan to call his mother to talk some sense into him. Mothers tend to know how to handle their sons better.

I decided to put distance between the tenants and me. I am looking into ways to avoid picking up the phone directly. Note: tenants are not your friends. Keep the distance.

John Paul Goatley, another fishbone in my throat, is now finally leaving. I had agreed to take John on just about three months ago; I was desperate to get the last single room at DOW14 rented. I took him on without doing my due diligence; a mistake that has now cost me some money and a lot of pain. John was the one that cut down all the trees in the garden the first week he moved in. John and Lloyd were the two Englishmen in the house. There were a Polish couple and a South African couple also in the house. The South African couple left because of the two men. I evicted Lloyd and another Polish couple moved in, so John was left without his partner in crime. He then put in his mind that the first Polish couple were now ganging up with the new Polish couple to kick him out and make the house a Polish haven.

John forgot that he was the troublemaker in the house. John smokes constantly in the house. I have caught him on numerous occasions and I had given him his final warning weeks before Lloyd was evicted. So when the new Polish couple called me two weeks after moving in, saying that John has been ignoring their request to stop smoking in the house, I went ballistic, and then issued him his eviction letter on the spot. I had already lost a good couple because of him; I was not prepared to lose another one.

John got in his mind that it was the two couples ganging up against him, so he went back to the house and attacked one of the girls. I was called immediately. I went to the house, took his keys, asked him to pack a night bag and I drove him to FIL949. The following morning, I got a van and moved all his stuff out of the house. I gave him a week to find another accommodation. I later discovered that he had mental issues too. He is schizophrenic. Anyway, tomorrow, John is finally leaving for good; hopefully, I will never hear anything from him ever again.

My observation so far in this business is that all my British tenants have turned out to be nightmares. Either they never want to pay, or they pay late, or they create havoc in the house. On the other side, all my foreign-born tenants have been fantastic. They are clean, they take care of the house, they do not expect me to wipe their butts, and they all pay me on time. The question for me now, based on my findings, is how do I avoid discrimination?

26 May 2011

Today I spoke with Tim's mother, the man from LOD47. She kindly apologised for her son's behaviour and explained to me that he had had a head injury a couple of years ago, which makes him incapable of thinking rationally in most cases. She asked me not to kick him out and to pass all bills to her from now on. I have not had any further problems with Tim since. He is now my longest tenant.

I also went to meet Frank at the b. & b. house to do the measurements for the future project. We caught up on the ways to finance the deal. The suggestion, to give the vendor 65 per cent now and then the remaining 35 per cent in six months' time, was refused by the vendor. She said she needed all the money up front. Steve, the finance guy's solution might have to wait in the pipeline while we try to get a mortgage. This means that we might have to come up with a 20 per cent deposit. We will know which way to go by Monday.

I moved in the third tenant at FIL949 today; one more and the house will be full.

By the way, this morning, David from FIL949 called to inform me that the toilet was no longer flushing. I immediately alerted the landlord, who promised to send someone in the morning. Later in the day, in the evening, David called again to inform me that the toilet had not been repaired, so I called the landlord again, she told me that someone had gone but had not fixed the problem.

I made my point clear that it needed to be done today. She then called back to say that she had found someone who was asking for £100; she asked me if we could share. I told her that the property was hers; therefore, the problem was also hers. How cheeky!

Brad of LOD47 is still running from paying his rent and Lee of BRE37 is avoiding paying his energy bill. What a cracker!

30 May 2011

All tenants have finally paid, except for Lee at the BRE37 property, with his energy bill.

The two single rooms at the DOW14 property have been snatched up by two Spanish men with whom I had been communicating on Easyroommate for the last two weeks. At the same time, a girl wanted one of the rooms for July. I promised to give her another room instead.

The last room in FIL949 was taken by a man I had also been communicating with for a week, a Frenchman working at Airbus, just few minutes' walk from the house.

The double room at BOS9 was taken by a couple who wished to move in straightaway but the room will only be available from 1 June. So I arranged for them to move into another room in Fishponds for a couple of days, then on 1 June, they can move into BOS9. The location is closer to their work.

The good times are arriving and the rooms are taken as they arrive on the market.

31 May 2011

As the last day of the month, I went to take the meter reading of all the properties. This usually takes three hours. This is also a time to catch up with the tenants, pick up the letters, and have a look at the general state of the house.

The single room at BOS9 was taken today by Addey, the girl who wanted to take the single at DOW14 a few days ago. She will move in on 1 July.

Kevin from KIM40 called to ask about the number of tenants in the house. He threatened to contact the council if I get in the last tenant for the single room. I have to point out here that KIM40 is a four-bedroom house, with two large doubles, one standard double, and a large single room. Kevin occupies one of the large doubles downstairs, Anica and Peter occupy the other one, Jakub and Evelina occupy the standard, and the large double is still vacant. Anyway, Kevin contacted me because he did not want more than five people in the house. I told him that it was not his business to tell me how to run my properties and that if he wanted to leave he was free to do so. Unbeknown to him, I have very good contacts with the council and the house is already a licenced HMO with two facilities.

I pointed out a few key points to him and kindly suggested he called the council to find out the facts.

It is amazing how tenants tend to react when it comes to having new people in the house. The best advice is to be aware of the *do*s and *don't*s because tenants will find a way to stick one to their landlords any time.

I called my contact at the council to update me with the rules and regulations, and as of today, I can have up to six people in the house.

2 June 2011

As of the beginning of this month, I decided to take a three-month break from taking on further properties. My plan during this period is to upgrade all my current properties by installing either TV or Freeview cable, painting and redecorating bathrooms, or clearing the gardens. The other plan is to clear off all bad tenants. This, I have managed to do by evicting Lloyd Lawson and John Goatley in May. In June are the turns of Joe from BOS1 and Lee from BRE37.

Joe has already given me his notice, so he should be out by 13 June, and Lee, who has been avoiding my calls for the past few weeks, will soon leave. There's been a commotion with him today which prompted me to change his locks and kick him out.

Lee is a tenant who couldn't find any accommodation when he approached me in January; he has failed to keep up with all his duties. Lee is the typical freeloader. No good deed ever goes unpunished.

Today, I bought Freeview cable for the DOW14 and FIL949 properties. The next upgrades were to redecorate the NEW61 bathroom and clear the BOS1 garden.

Graham was contacted to solve the problem of the bathroom shower at FIL949 house. The shower had no pressure and the tenants complained about it. Fortunately, he had a spare electric shower in his van so the problem was resolved in a heartbeat. He only charged the cost of the shower. When I told the landlady about this, she was very grateful. I saved her over 50 per cent of the usual cost. She paid only £172 instead of £269 for the shower and £80 installation fee. I also took the opportunity to upgrade the shower from 8-kilowatt to 9.8-kilowatt.

Graham is also part of my Master Mind Team. A good tradesperson is worth gold.

3 June 2011

The first thing I did this morning was to go to BRE37 to change Lee's locks. I met Graham and his apprentice there. As I approached Lee's room, I realised that his door was open and I found out that he had vacated the house. That made my day. He had also left his keys.

After a few hours, I had the hunch to call the tenants and ask them if he had left anything behind. Paul, his next-door neighbour, admitted that he had left a few things, including his flat-screen TV and a speaker. So I took those. I now have something to hold onto until he pays what he owes.

I went to the NEW61 house to put a cleaning notice in their kitchen and to clean up the mouldy bathroom; it took a bottle of bleach to work the magic.

It seems like as soon as I get one trouble maker out another one arises. I am now having issues with Kevin, the new tenant at KIM40. For some reason, he has decided to take upon himself the cause of applying the law on HMOs. He has been bothering me all week about getting a sixth tenant into the house. I have a room still available there and he is campaigning with the other tenants to keep it empty. I told him to go ahead with his campaign and also that he should join the council in trying to find an accommodation for a couple I was helping out at that moment in the house.

The couple is Jakub and Evelina who were expecting their first child. I took them on because they were almost homeless.

4 June 2011

Today, I spent some time preparing the very large double room at NEW61 house. Two couples came over to view it; unfortunately, they had time on their hands and were not planning to move before the end of June.

Alexander from Kazakhstan arrived today straight from his country. He enrolled for a month's course at the local EF language school. He arrived with just a suitcase. I decided to show him around Fishpond area. I gave him the last room at KIM40. Before he arrived, I had had a meeting with the tenants, except Kevin, the trouble maker, who was not around. The tenants had no problem with the room being let, and why should they?

I drove Alexander to get his SIM card and some food for the night. I also showed him where to take his bus to his school. He asked me if I usually did that, and I told him that it was definitely not the case, but I understood what it was to be new in a country.

In the evening, I mailed out an update to my entire contact list.

KIM40 tenants needed an additional fridge for the house. I found a second hand repairman who sells his repairs on Gumtree. I contacted him and will visit him on Monday. He could be another one to add to my Master Mind team.

5 June 2011

Today, Sunday, I did a bit more of marketing for my bulk viewings of BOS71 and DOU54 on Thursday. I already had quite a few people who were interested. I believed all the rooms would be taken by the end of that week. These were the two properties I had found in February and had paid for in May. Sometimes when a good bargain comes up, it is worth the wait. BOS71 is a four-bedroom house and DOU54 is a five-bedroom house, both HMO licensed. DOU54 was made into a six-bedroom shared house as it has two facilities. Profit went from £700 to £1,000 by doing that.

6 June 2011

The KIM40 tenants had asked for a fridge on Saturday, I managed to get a second hand one for them by Monday. I found an engineer on Gumtree who fixes electrical appliances. So I saw his wife this morning and I bought a large fridge for just £70 including delivery. That was a bargain.

I showed the room at BRE37 to a man whose name is Aaron from New Zealand. He seems quite interested; perhaps he will take it.

I sent a text to Lee, the man who ran away from BRE37. I discovered that he had left his bike and more stuff behind, so I told him that they were all in my care and he needed to come and get them within the next twenty-four hours, otherwise I would charge him a fee of £5 per day. I also specified that they would be released as long as he pays his £108 energy bill and his rent arrears too. He said he would report me to the police because what I was doing was illegal, I told him they were already aware and that he was running for a reason. I told him only thieves run away and only crooks try to dodge their responsibilities. I told him he was one or the other; he did not reply after that. And I never saw him again.

I am heavily marketing the DOU54 and BOS71 rooms and I am receiving good feedback. I am expecting most of the rooms to be taken by the end of the week. The single room at BOS71 has already been paid for by a man who resides in Cheshire. Three rooms are already pre-booked by a group of three workers coming from Hungary. One double room at DOU54 is also pre-booked.

All that before I even get the keys to the houses: Looking good.

7 June 2011

Just to stay on the safe side of things, I decided to send a non-renewal letter to Kevin, as below:

Letter to Kevin:

Dear Mr Borowskyj 07 May 2011

As per your contract, which terminates on 25 July 2011, we are writing to inform you that we will not be renewing this agreement. This means that you will have to vacate the room by 25 July 2011, leave it in the same state as you found it when you moved in, and return the keys.

Your energy bill will be calculated and passed on to you. You can pay whichever way suits you.

For any comments, please submit then in writing to our office at Victoria St, BS1.

Regards

Taiwo Orishayomi

STAK PI Ltd

After sending the above letter, I headed to London for my VIP meeting with the Duo. I spent the whole day on buses and trains. Whilst in the public transportations, I used my time to send bulk emails to my entire list; some responded, but most didn't.

I will send another reminder tomorrow.

8 June 2011

On my way back to Bristol, I sent another batch reminder to my list. I had more success this time; I received about seven confirmations, mostly for the evening viewing.

I came back from London and went home to catch up on the previous day's marketing workload.

I spent the next couple of hours reading emails and responding to them.

After that, I went to collect the keys for BOS71 and DOU54. The DOU54 house carpet was in very bad condition, something I would point out to the agent. I will request it be changed.

I then went to do Aaron's contract for BRE37. Aaron had called me this morning to tell me he wanted the room. Then I ran to NEW61 to show the large double room to Zoe; she loved it and took it straight away. It was funny that when I arrived at NEW61 house, one of the tenants was baking a cake, which gave a very lovely and homey smell to the whole house. It was a secret trick to sell a home quickly that I had heard on TV one day. The smell of warm cake fresh from the oven makes buyers want to buy.

Tomorrow, I do the new houses.

9 June 2011

Today was my first day of bulk viewings at both BOS71 and DOU54. Fortunately, I had some help from my mother who came for a few days of training. I was at BOS71 while she was at DOU54.

Out of seven confirmations, only three turned up.

I later went to the landlord exhibition at the University of West England. We made some very useful contacts, on which I will follow up. I met Geoff, my other business partner and we ran through the course notes again. I had set a target for August to start doing the courses. This is another way of supplementing the income.

13 June 2011

Jakub and Evelina, the couple I had tried to help had missed their payments again. Their excuse was that I had many houses; I could therefore afford to give them a free accommodation. Sometimes we just have to admit that sometimes good intentions backfire. I have tried to speak sense to them but to no avail. So I decided to give them a deadline instead. The letter is hereby attached.

Final request for payment owed. 13 June 2011

Dear Jakub and Evelina,

Due to your unsatisfactory first month at KIM40, we have decided that it would be better for you to look for a more affordable accommodation.

Despite our reduction in rent from £375pcm to £350 pcm, you are still unable to make your regular weekly rent payment without needing a constant reminder. As a company, we only look to work with trustworthy tenants, a quality you have failed to demonstrate.

Please bear in mind that your situation has nothing to do with us. As adults, we all have our duties and responsibilities. Ours is to maintain the house, pay insurances, pay taxes, and pay our mortgage. Yours is to pay your rent and bills on time.

You have been living in the house for one month and one week. By now, we should have received:

A one-month deposit of £350

One month's rent: £350

One week's rent of £82

Total: £782

So far, we have received bits and pieces:

£170 paid upon moving in

£82 bank transfer

£41 cash

£80 cash

£166 bank transfer

Total: £539

To avoid eviction, you will have to pay your weekly rent of £82 promptly and make three instalments towards your deposit for the next three weeks.

Friday 17 June: £171

Friday 24 June: £170

Friday 1 July: £170

Thereafter: £82 weekly

The above does not include your energy bill, which also must be paid promptly. If you fail to honour the above payments, you will be issued an official eviction letter, which will be applicable within two months. You will also incur all charges and expenses relating to your eviction.

Taiwo Orishayomi

STAK PI Ltd

14 May 2011

Today was a day of sitting in for Virgin Media connection at the BOS71 house and the carpet fitters' measurement for DOU54. Whilst waiting for the tradesmen to arrive, I went to BOS9 to sort out Joe Bradley's moving out paperwork. His room was satisfactory, so we signed the waiver form and took the meter readings, and I took his keys back.

When I got home, I received an email from Andrea who had apparently left the house suddenly. My guess was that she and her husband and Joe had moved in together and she had purposely left without giving notice. I have her deposit.

I also hand-delivered Jakub's final notice, and posted the first bill for KIM40. Not surprisingly, Kevin, the troublemaker, texted me to ask why the calculation was seven pence more than the bill. All calculation figures are rounded up.

I have asked Geoff to call Jakub tomorrow to give him a man-to-man talk as he seems to be taking me for a ride.

Again, no good deed goes unpunished. I now realise that tenants will lie and cheat on a landlord the minute they no longer need his or her accommodation. Be careful not to give in too much to tenants' requests. The more you give, the more they ask for. Stick to the basic needs and they should provide themselves with the rest. Tenants want all luxuries for nothing. And again, who does not?

15 June 2011

Today I sent a message to all my tenants regarding jobs. I have associated my company with GM's new maintenance company called Quinn Associates. I saw that they were constantly looking for workers, i.e. cleaners, painters, decorators, etc., so I arranged for all the jobs to come to me first. The plan is to pass them on to my tenants. The majority of my tenants are foreign professionals looking for work. The idea is to help them get jobs, hence be able to pay their rents, and be grateful to my company in a way, and stay longer.

I went to Ikea today to buy two TV stands, which cost me £16. This was for the BOS71 house. I also bought some cleaning materials for FIL949. Some little low-cost touches make a big difference.

21 June 2011

So what do you do when your car breaks down? That was exactly my day today. I had to cancel all my viewings and reschedule them for tomorrow. Luckily, the potential tenants were all fine.

I sent emails to Mahesh, the new property manager with whom I now had to work. Grenger Group seemed not to care about how they manage their new role, which they took over from GM. DOU54 was given to me with no works done. I had to fight to get the carpet changed and deal with the leak problems in the kitchen. I was stuck with a house I could not let out until the problems were solved.

I asked GG, Mahesh, to start my contract from the day they solve the problems, to which he persistently said no. I had to think about taking the matter further.

I have now reduced the prices of DOU54 rooms to £350 pcm each as I have decided to transform the lounge into a big room, charging £375 pcm for it. I now have quite a few interested people; hopefully all rooms will be let by the end of the month.

22 June 2011

I received a couple of calls today from Italy and France. A forty-year-old Italian woman wanted to take the big room at DOU54. When she called, she kept mentioning a couple of blue pillows in the picture of the room. Then she confirmed that she wanted to take it, but asked for pictures of the garden and other angles of the room. When I sent her those, she came back to tell me that the blue pillows were not there; therefore, she didn't want it any longer; how strange some people are. She probably thought she was going to a hotel.

Three French girls also contacted me from Easyroommate. They wanted me to reserve three rooms at the DOU54 property for them when they arrived on the thirtieth. I told them I needed to have some form of deposit to hold the rooms for so long. I never heard anything from them again.

Experience has taught me never to hold anything for someone who is abroad and not willing to commit him or herself while asking you to commit your room. They usually will not show up, or on rare occasions when they do show up, they will walk away with an apology, "I'm sorry but this is not what I expected". But you saw the pictures!

23 June 2011

DOU54 house repairs are still going on. The dishwasher was leaking and the whole kitchen floor is wet. The humidity attracted an infestation of slugs into the house. I had to put down anti slug poison. The following day, I had a dozen dead slugs in a corner of the kitchen. It was disgusting!

The new lino had to be taken out, the wet floor drained, and all appliances pulled out and left to dry over the weekend. This house is going to make me £1,008 pcm profit; this is why I am still holding onto it. I took some pictures, which will be passed on to GG. I will use this information to retain the first month's rent. I have not been able to rent the property due to all the repairs that should have been done before getting the keys.

24 June 2011

As I expected, Jakub and Evelina could not follow their rent schedule. The man called me again yesterday to tell me that his tax code still had not been changed and that he could only pay £150 out of the £170 he owes me. Again, I should not have allowed someone who cannot pay for the house in the first place: My fault.

Joe Bradley, the man who wanted to have a cat at the BOS9 property, texted me in a rude manner again. I just ignored him. He wanted to know if the bill had arrived so he could get the rest of his deposit back. I told him it had not. He then threatened to contact Andrews, the agency from whom I am renting the place. I told him to go ahead. He then responded by saying how unprofessional I was. This was funny, coming out of the mouth of a man who had never paid his rent in full or on time. I told him he was wasting my time and that the procedure laid down in the waiver form shall be followed.

Most of my rooms were taken within few days. I rented out one room yesterday, three the day before, and one today. I had six out of eleven rooms left. They were all rented by the end of the month.

I am now charging every tenant a £30 fee for my deposit scheme. And I am considering making all bills inclusive in the rent. It is less hassle for me and for them. This just means that the rent will be higher than the market rate.

25 June 2011

Today three tenants moved in; Addey into BOS9, and Sanchez and Joe into DOU54. Tomorrow, Benoit and Riccardo will also move into DOU54.

I had a couple viewing BOS9 today. They were artists; the man was a painter and the girl a poet. They looked, sounded, and behaved like stoned artists. They had a set of questions ready for me, which I gladly answered. They went away and called back after an hour to say that they would like to take the room. I gave them a second appointment to pay the deposit and take details.

Ela had come to see DOW14 yesterday. She loved the house because most of the housemates were from her country. Ela was having troubles with her current housemate, apparently a bully policewoman who loved lots of lights but could not be bothered to go out of her room for natural light. Instead, she would turn on all the lights in the house and in her room, wasting energy, which she had to share among the rest of the tenants. Ela came with her best friend, who didn't look friendly at all; she spoke with the tenants again and decided to go for it. I had just two rooms at DOU54 and one room at BOS71 currently empty. Riccardo had been working hard to get me tenants for DOU54. He got £20 for each tenant that signed a contract.

27 June 2011

Riccardo from DOU54 did it again. He found me another tenant for the house. For that, he was rewarded handsomely with £20. Alberto, one of the mates at the language school, came this evening to have a look at the room, and he took it; just one more room to go.

My mad tenant, Kevin, struck again. I texted him to let him know about a viewing for tonight and he texted me back asking for twenty-four hours' notice to access the house. I told him that he could keep access to his room but as a shared house, he did not own the communal areas.

So when my viewing arrived at 8.30 p.m., he refused to allow any access into the house. I gently pushed him out of my way, something he was not very happy about, and he started cursing. My guest went into the garden and—my mistake—I followed him. Kevin immediately locked us outside, then went to the front door, and did the same. I called Alex, one of the tenants, to open the door, but Kevin refused him any access. The man was scheduled to leave on 25 July. I could not wait to see that happen.

CHAPTER III

SYSTEM ESTABLISHED

Taking Advantage of the Economic Crash

July-September 2011

I did a lot of house cleaning; by this, I mean I removed all troublesome tenants in order to get ready for the September rush. I discovered that in my area, the months of September and October represent the gold rush for all local landlords. The university students start a new academic year. The teachers arrive from all over the world. Large employers bring in new staff for work that lasts between six months and a year, and many previous contracts end so many people tend to look for new homes.

I took the months of July and August off. I went on a five-day holiday to the south of France, but I could not relax one bit. I had worked very hard for many months, and I found it hard to wind down. So I decided to spend my energy cleaning my friends' house and devouring books in their library.

1 September 2011

I took over BOS78. I now have four houses on the same street. Anything that comes up there is mine.

21 October 2011

It has been over three months since I stopped my daily recap. Many things have happened since then. I have acquired more properties, giving me a total of fourteen houses: almost seventy tenants to manage. Riccardo from DOU54 now works full time with me. His enthusiasm is equally that of mine.

The joint venture with the Wolleys failed when they requested 60 per cent of the b. & b. deal I had found. They had been some of my very first students. The strategy I had taught them was stolen and given to the Duo. My relationship with the Duo fell to pieces at the same time. The humiliation came when my strategy was presented in front of all the VIP members whilst I was there. My name was not mentioned. All credit was given to the Wolleys. The Duo knowingly denied any knowledge of what had happened. They simply said to me that I did not invent the strategy. I knew I did not invent it, but I brought it to their attention and I taught it to them and the Wolleys. I bury the whole affair in this short paragraph.

On a brighter note though, my joint venture with Geoff Whittaker is going from strength to strength. Our course is on track to start on 22 November 2011. We are now in the process of registering our trademark and launching ourselves into the world of courses.

This month, I took my very first company dividend of £6,000; it is good to see the rewards of hard work.

This month also, I took on one of my biggest properties, an eight-bedroom Victorian mansion just off Gloucester Road. All the rooms were taken within two weeks. Here goes the breakdown:

Rent of house: £1,100 pcm

Bills: £208 pcm

Very large room 1: £475 pcm

Very large room 2: £465 pcm

Very large room 3: £450 pcm

Double room 1: £360 pcm

Double room 2: £350 pcm

Double room 3: £350 pcm

Double room 4: £330 pcm

Single room 1: £200 pcm

Gross profit: £2,980 pcm

Net profit: £1,672 pcm

Net profit per annum: £20,064 (higher than the average salary or pension)

This house is the most profitable of all my houses. The secret is to take the lounge out and make it into an additional bedroom. This guarantees a "no party" house and more money coming in.

I have to point out here that although this house is bringing in a massive amount of profit it also cost me some dough to put it right. I spent four solid days painting the walls, installing the curtains, and building desks, wardrobes and chairs from scratch. The gain is worth the pain for sure. I will also change one of the bathrooms completely. My handyman Graham has secured a good deal for me and it will only cost me £400 for a new coat of white. This alone will allow me to increase the rent a little bit.

When the number of properties starts to rise, it is advisable to put systems in place immediately. Ideally, one has to coach someone else to do the same job. If you can show someone else how to do your job, then you have a system. One of the systems I was advised about by my accountant was to have a house reference for all rent payments so that I know exactly what each house is costing me and how much income each house is bringing in. My house reference system goes as follows: The first three letters of the house plus the house number.

The other system I have put in place is the format of all my advertisements. This stands out and people know me under the pseudonym of Lauren Marshall. Lauren Marshall has her way of writing and presenting her properties. This format comes with an up-to-date series of pictures of each room and house. Many people have even told me that they recognise and trust my advertisements when they see them. Some examples of my ads are as follows:

Fishponds rooms

Location: Fishponds, BS16

Room type: A large double

Rate: £385 pcm

Available: 25 July 2011

Hi,

I have a standard double room available in Fishponds; £325 pcm. The room is in a five-bedroom professional house. The Big Morrisons super market and Lidl are just close by.

The house is close to Frenchay and UWE.

The room is fully furnished with a double bed, a desk and chair, and a wardrobe.

The house comprises:

- Lounge
- Fully furnished kitchen
- Dishwasher
- Washing machine/dryer
- One bathroom
- Garden
- Free parking
- Wireless broadband
- Weekly cleaner
- Most bills inclusive (Council Tax, TV licence, water, broadband)
- Gas and electricity are shared among all tenants.

All rooms are for professionals or house trained students only. No pets or children allowed.

If you wish to view one of our rooms, please contact me on 07000000000.

Other available rooms in a four-bedroom house off Gloucester Rd:

Large double (couple okay): £455 pcm

Standard double: £400 pcm

Single: Now let

Kind regards

Lauren

*   *   *

Hi,

I have a very large double for £460 pcm available in Fishponds. The room is in a four-bedroom professional house. The Big Morrisons and Lidl are just close by.

The room is fully furnished with a double bed, a desk, a chair, and a wardrobe.

Good location for UWE, Frenchay campus.

The house comprises:

- Lounge
- Fully furnished kitchen
- Dishwasher
- Washing machine
- One Bathroom
- Garden
- Free parking
- Wireless broadband
- Weekly cleaner
- Most bills inclusive (Council Tax, TV licence, water, broadband)
- Gas and electricity are shared among all tenants.

All rooms are for professionals or house trained students only. No pets or children allowed.

This is suitable for a couple.

If you wish to view one of our rooms, please contact me on 07000000000.

Kind regards

Lauren

* * *

BRE37

Location: BS16

Available: Immediately

Price: £360 pcm

This standard double room is available in Fishponds. It is in a five-bedroom house located near St Matts (UWE). The house benefits from a sunroom, which opens into the lounge so you can still enjoy the outdoors on rainy days.

The house is close to local amenities. The Big Morrisons and Lidl are just close by.

The room is fully furnished with wireless Internet.

The house comprises:

- Lounge
- Sun room
- Fully furnished kitchen
- Dishwasher
- Washing machine/dryer
- Garden
- Free parking
- Wireless broadband
- Weekly cleaner
- Most bills inclusive (Council Tax, TV licence, water, broadband)
- Gas and electricity are shared among all tenants.

To reserve a viewing, just contact me on 07000000000.

* * *

FIL949

Hi

I have one double room in Filton, five minutes' walk to Airbus and Rolls Royce, ten minutes; drive to Bradley Stoke and Aztec West.

Frenchay, UWE and MOD are just close by. Bike it, walk it, drive it, or hop on a bus to your desired destination.

Several buses go straight into the city centre.

There is easy parking in front of the house.

The house comprises:

- Fully furnished lounge
- Fully furnished kitchen
- Washing machine
- Garden
- Free parking
- Wardrobe, single or double bed in each room
- Wireless Internet
- Most bills inclusive (Council Tax, TV licence, water, broadband)
- Gas and electricity are shared among all tenants

Double room 2: £360 pcm (available from 10 September 2011)

All rooms are for professionals or house trained students only. No pets or children allowed.

Kind regards

Lauren

*   *   *

As you can see, I only invest in three or four postcode areas. The reason is I do not want to scatter my houses all over the place. Keep it concise to keep the control. By doing this, you save yourself time, energy and money.

Financial Freedom: September-November 2011

The good thing about this strategy is that anyone can do it. I have helped several struggling landlords to solve their problems. I have helped several would-be property owners to save enough to get on the property ladder.

When I hear about banks repossessing homes, I do not understand why those struggling landlords cannot simply transform their lounge into an extra room and rent it out. There are many foreign students arriving in the UK every day, looking for affordable accommodation in a family: The accommodation is cheap, and they get to stay in an English family to practice the language. Landlords could be family hosts and make money by acting as such.

The legalities of renting out parts of their homes scare many people. As long as the landlord lives in the house, there are no rules forbidding him or her from renting. All you need is a licence agreement between you and the tenant.

If you wish to move out of the house completely and rent it, all you need is an agreement from your mortgage lender that allows you to do so. As far as my mortgage lender is concerned, I only need to pay £200 and I have the right to rent out my house. Where I live, my house is worth £695 pcm but with my strategy, I can get £1,000 pcm, as I mentioned at the beginning of the book. This does only cover my new mortgage of £555 pcm, but I also have a profit of £495 pcm!

I have lifted the legal meanings from LandlordZONE, to better explain the difference between a licence and an AST (Assured Shorthold Tenancy Agreement).

What is a Tenancy?

A tenancy is an "estate in land" granted for a determined period of time—"term of years" or "fixed-term".

For example: a tenancy may be 6 months,1 year, 21 years, 99 years etc.

Alternatively a tenancy may be granted for a specific shorter period—a periodic tenancy—yearly, monthly, weekly, even daily).

In return for the "time limited" but *exclusive use* and possession of the land (and any building/s on that land) the tenant pays his landlord *rent*.

The landlord may be the freeholder (owner for life—life tenant) or a tenant herself; e.g.:

Freeholder (owner) Landlord grants tenancy to:

—Tenant A (head lease holder)

—Tenant A grants a tenancy to "B" (sublease holder)

—Tenant B grants a tenancy to "C" etc.

So long as each subsequent *sublease* is shorter in length than the previous one there is no problem.

A tenancy gives a tenant a "legal interest in the land" and he or she cannot easily be deprived of that interest by the landlord. The landlord would need good reason to terminate the tenancy (breach of contract) and would ordinarily need a court order to do so.

To all intents and purposes, whilst a tenancy is in force, the tenant occupier is the *owner of the land* and can act as any other owner would, so long as it's within the terms of his lease agreement and current statutory requirements (Acts of Parliament).

Tenants have a right to *"quiet enjoyment"* which means the freedom to enjoy the property as any "owner" would—free from unnecessary interference by the landlord.

Tenancy agreements are partly contractual, i.e. an *agreement between landlord and tenant* which can be enforced by a court of law. They are also controlled in England and Wales by long established common law property laws. And, particularly with residential tenancies (as opposed to commercial or business tenancies), they are partly governed by *statutory* (Parliamentary) *rules,* which cannot be over-ridden by the contractual common law rules.

An important point to remember is that *residential* tenancy agreement terms must be deemed **"fair"** by the *Unfair Terms in Consumer Contracts Regulations 1999.* See the Office of Fair Trading's *Guide to Unfair Terms in Tenancy Agreements.*

An unfair term in a tenancy agreement may well reassure the landlord, or indeed the tenant, on some point, but it would be *unenforceable at law.*

Fixed Term & Periodic Tenancies

Tenancies usually start with an *agreed fixed-term,* (for example 6 or 12 months) during which time both parties are contractually bound—the tenant to *pay rent for the full term,* and the landlord to allow the tenant exclusive possession and quiet enjoyment.

Once the *fixed-term* of a tenancy has expired, however, unless a new fixed-term is agreed, all tenancies automatically become *periodic tenancies.* These are based on the rent payment period—*weekly or monthly* etc. The periodic tenancy can thus continue until one side, landlord or tenant, gives notice.

At the end of the fixed-term the tenant can leave, but if he or she stays on, even for just one day, a periodic tenancy is automatically created—there is no legal requirement for either party to do anything at all—the tenancy can *continue on indefinitely* on a periodic basis and on exactly the same terms as the original agreement, which still fully applies.

What is a Licence?

A tenancy gives the tenant a legal interest in the land—in effect, legal ownership for the period of the tenancy. The tenancy can even be sold (assigned) to another tenant, though residential tenancies usually forbid this.

The *grant of a license* does not create an estate in land and the licensee does not gain an interest in the property, purely permission to occupy it. Stays in Hotels, Hostels, Lodgings (where the "landlord" is resident but the tenant does not have exclusive possession of any part) letting a room in your own home, holiday lettings, employees of a business living on the premises, and some houses in Multiple Occupation (HMOs) are all license agreements. See Licenses.

Occupier with Basic Protection—Common Law Tenancy

Interestingly, there is in fact a half-way house between tenant (full tenancy rights) and lodger (licence to occupy)—it's call an "Occupier with *basic protection*" or a Common Law Tenancy. This situation arises where the tenant shares a house or building with the landlord, but not the accommodation, and has exclusive possession of one part, normally a self-contained flat. In this situation the tenant is a common law tenant having reduced protection as compared to a tenant or tenants occupying a separate property with an Assured Shorthold (Housing Acts 1988 & 1996) tenancy. With a Common Law Residential Tenancy any deposit taken is not subject to the Deposit Protection rules and the complicated Housing Act possession procedures. The landlord can merely forfeit the tenancy for breach of contract.

Long Tenancies or Leases

Residential landlords are mainly concerned with letting on short tenancies (up to 7 years) but if they let out flats they may themselves have bought a long lease on the flat—usually anything up to 999 years.

A long lease involves the purchase or payment of a premium (purchase price of the lease) along with usually an annual ground rent and service charges. See Long-Leasehold.

Multiple Tenants

When more than one residential tenant occupies a property it is common to have all the individuals sign the lease agreement (Joint Tenancy) so that all have *joint and several* liability. If one tenant absconds, all the others, or if the landlord can find only one, just one of the others, is responsible for all the rent and expenses.

Tenants should ensure that their sharers in a joint tenancy are responsible people, or they may find themselves footing the bill!

Creating a Tenancy

A tenancy can be created by the conduct of the parties and does not need to have a written agreement to be legally binding.

Once a person is given possession (exclusively) of land or property (usually evidenced by possession of the keys) and the owner accepts rent payments, a tenancy comes into existence.

Creating tenancies on a casual basis such as this (even for friends, perhaps especially for friends) is not the sort of thing any sensible landlord would do! A written agreement or lease is absolutely crucial to any successful tenant / landlord relationship.

Any landlord (or tenant) without a written agreement is "in the lap of the gods" or, more specifically, the civil court judges. The relationship is then governed entirely by whatever statutory rules exist and the ability to provide evidence other than a written agreement as to the rent payable, when it is due, and when the tenancy started.

Modern agreements aim to strike a fair balance between the interests of both the tenant and the landlord and should be in plain English.

It's good practice for landlords to make sure that tenants understand their agreements (obligations) at the signing of the agreement, by discussing the terms.

Tenants in any doubt should seek legal advice, though reputable "standard" residential tenancy agreements often afford some reassurance.

Tenancy Agreement or Lease?

Ordinary written residential tenancy agreements can be bought "off the shelf" from various sources. See the LandlordZONE Agreements and Documents sections.

So long as these agreements have been well drafted they often suffice quite nicely for residential tenancies. Experienced landlords and agents often like to include specific clauses of their own, and may have them prepared by a solicitor.

An ordinary written agreement cannot be used for a tenancy exceeding *three years in length*. Tenancies for longer periods need a *lease* drawn up and signed as a deed.

What kind of Residential Tenancy?

There are currently 5 kinds of residential tenancies:

1. The *Protected (Rent Act) Tenancy*—tenancies entered into before 15 January 1989.

2. The *Assured Tenancy*—introduced by the Housing Act 1988.

3. The Assured Tenancy—Housing Act 1988

4. The *Assured Shorthold Tenancy*—introduced in 1988 but amended by the 1996 Housing Act.

5. The Common Law Tenancy—as explained above, where landlord live in the same building

The Rent Act Tenancy

These tenancies give the residential tenant considerable security of tenure and they also regulate the level of rent payable by the tenant.

Basically these are uneconomic to operate and landlords need to exercise caution when purchasing properties with existing tenants (sitting tenants), in case there are any Rent Act tenants.

As a general guide a property with a sitting Rent Act tenant is worth considerably less than its vacant possession value. These properties regularly go through auctions as "reversionary investments, where landlord investors purchase for their reversion value, expecting to gain when the sitting tenant passes on. It is important to realise here that under the Rent Act rules members of the tenants family, in some circumstances, have succession rights to the tenancy.

The Residential Property Tribunal Service can determine Fair Rents and Market rents for Regulated (Rent Act) and Assured tenancies.

The Assured Tenancy

The modern assured tenancy still affords tenants security of tenure but enables the landlord to charge a market rent and to regain possession on certain grounds, as laid down in the Housing Act 1988. For example, if the tenant falls behind in his rent payments by more than 2 months the landlord can apply to the courts for a possession order.

The Residential Property Tribunal Service determine Fair rents and Market rents for Regulated (Rent Act) and Assured tenancies.

The Assured Shorthold Tenancy

A special kind of Assured Tenancy is the Assured Shorthold which has one additional special ground for possession—it is a guaranteed granting of a possession order after an initial agreed period (the shorthold period) of usually 6 months.

All new tenancies since 28 February 1997 are automatically Assured Shortholds, unless the agreement has specified an Assured Tenancy.

Shorthold Tenancies granted after 15 January 1989 and before 28 February 1997 are only enforceable by the landlord if the correct notice was served at start. A prescribed form Section 20 Notice was needed.

Point to Watch for Landlords

1. Once a tenancy has been created, it cannot be changed to another type of tenancy by or on renewal.

2. Rent Act Tenancies can seriously damage your wealth and perhaps your health as well!

3. Beware when buying properties with sitting tenants. Are there any Rent Act tenants?

4. If there are early Shorthold tenants, has a *Section 20 Notice* been properly served, can you prove it, and does a proper Shortlhold agreement exist?

5. Never, ever create a tenancy on a casual basis—always have a substantial written agreement which is properly witnessed on signing.

6. Make sure that all occupants in your property are documented tenants, having signed an agreement. New arrivals should be put on the agreement as soon as possible.

7. Never try to force a tenant to leave—a court possession order must always be obtained if the tenant won't leave and the landlord wishes to end a tenancy—see Harassment.

8. If in doubt about the financial security of the tenant or for younger tenants always try to obtain a surety agreement (guarantee) from parents or another home-owner willing to stand surety in case of default or damage.

9. Always screen and verify tenants very carefully before handing over the keys to your property. Remember, you are handing over a very valuable asset when you let out your property—would a bank lend you money without doing thorough checks?

Tenancies brought into existence before 15 January 1989 are governed by the Rent Act 1977. These are uneconomic for landlords to operate—avoid them if you can. Exercise extreme caution when purchasing properties with existing tenants.

Tenancies commencing after 15 January 1989 but before 28 February 1997 may be either Assured Tenancies or Assured Shorthold Tenancies. The default tenancy here is the Assured one which offers more security to the tenant, unless the landlord can show that the correct Shorthold (Section 20) Notice was served. Again, caution is needed when purchasing with existing tenants.

After 28 February 1997 the default tenancy is the Assured Shorthold Tenancy. This is unless the landlord served a notice specifically stating that an Assured Tenancy was being created.

Useful websites

LandlordZONE <www.landlordzone.co.uk>: This is very good to find out about the legislation regarding the property industry in the UK. You can become a member for free. My advice to you is to join.

The websites of your local council, tenant/landlord division: Your local council is your bank of free advice. Use them as much as you can. You pay for the service every month anyway, so why not take advantage of it? Make sure you befriend somebody in that department. Go back to them as many times as you can. Get to meet them face-to-face too. Make them feel useful. This advice alone is worth *gold*!

Legal Centre.co.uk <www.legalcentre.co.uk>: This website has enabled me to buy a standard AST and licence to occupy forms which I edit accordingly. This is the best for all your legal documents without having to pay a fortune.

Chapter IV

Collaborations, Setbacks, and New Horizons

My collaboration with Geoff Whittaker is now getting off the ground after some months of standing still. The wakeup call came along when my strategy was presented at the Duo's VIP meeting a few weeks ago. The humiliation was uncanny. The Wolleys were on stage presenting my course word for word. There was nothing authentic and every single bit of it was exactly what I had taught them. Bob, one of the Duo, was informed but avoided any chance of discussing the matter. He even had the guts to ask me to pay £3,500 to join his Graduate Program. I got nothing from the VIP I paid for last year, so why should I join the grads?

Bob also informed me that he would have JVed with me if I had approached him before the Wolleys. Why would I have wanted to JV with him when I knew that the best I would have gotten out of the deal was 30 per cent: 30 per cent for me and 70 per cent for him? The perfect example is Terry Cootmore, a very good lease option trainer. For some reason he decided to go into a JV partnership with Bob. He was only paid £100 for a full day training twenty-odd students who had paid £1,000 each to be there. I would rather work on my own. Even if I were to get only one student a month, I would still walk away with a profit higher than the average salary in this country.

At this stage, a year down the line, I have become a lot cleverer in this business. You have probably noticed this too. I have met sharks and saints along the way. The sharks have made me stronger and the saints have made me grounded and humble.

This strategy is very simple, but human beings make the simplest things very complicated. The truth is that you need to make the landlords feel comfortable. You need them more than they need you, should the truth be spoken. The letting market is strong, unlike the buying market. Also, beware of people who talk the talk but cannot walk the walk. You will find many in this industry. Sharks will exploit you; there are many of them out there. Do not allow manipulators to take advantage of you. I have paid for some courses with some so-called gurus whom I thought were actually doing what they were coaching. I finally discovered that in fact, they were just vomiting what someone else had taught them. This is why I always show facts and figures, including my bank statements, at my training courses. I am still taking on properties as of today. What I coach is what I do every single day.

2 November 2011

Geoff and I travelled to Peterborough to film our first YouTube video for the launch of our website. We filmed three videos presenting the strategy and introducing our webinar. The videos will be released one at a time. The branding of our company will be video based. This will allow our site to be rated high on Google search engine. Google owns YouTube, so this is a lot easier and cheaper than SEO campaigns.

4 November 2011

I got the keys to my fourteenth property today. It is a five-bedroom house, unfurnished, with a lounge. The lounge is automatically transformed into an additional bedroom to avoid parties in the house. Potential profit on that one is £900 pcm. Riccardo and I will spend the next few days buying furniture from IKEA and building them. We intend to rent the whole lot by the end of next week.

The business is growing at a high speed now, so Riccardo needs a car. My course with Geoff is now taking off; we have two mentoring sessions booked for early December, and we got two delegates without advertising!

As soon as Riccardo gets his car, he will be handling all the daily tasks on Bristol-Rentals while I focus on the courses. The secret is to get the business systematized at an early stage so that I do not have to be involved on a daily basis. This is the advice many business owners give. It is hard for me to delegate as I have grown this business from scratch. I have to if I want to expand elsewhere.

6 November 2011

Car shopping today; we need an estate car that is big enough to take double beds. This will save us money and make running the business easier.

We found nothing worthwhile buying. We need a VW Passat Estate, which will enable us to transport heavy furniture. So far, I have had to rely on using the service of a friend with a van. My accountant suggests leasing a car instead of buying one outright.

7 November 7, 2011

I received a very surprising phone call from Glenn Armstrong, one of the leading property gurus in the UK. A friend of mine knows him personally. This friend also knows about my recent troubles with the Duo, so he decided to introduce me to Glenn. Glenn called me and asked me, "Do you believe in faith?" I responded yes, but added that sometimes, we do make our own faith.

He asked me if I could come to the event he would be hosting the following weekend. A speaking spot became available and he wanted me to be the speaker. When one door shuts down two others tend to open up. This is just the case for me. The Duo stole my strategy and £497 of my money, a down payment towards a speaking course, which they now refuse to refund me. Now, I am going to be speaking on the same stage as Jim

Haliburton, Paul Ribbons, and other leading property experts in the UK. I would even be introduced by Juswant, the owner of Berkshire Property Meet! How great is that?

8 November 2011

I have been working with Niq, Glenn's assistant, to organise my presentation. I will have one hour on the stage and fifteen minutes of Q&A.

Good thing I already had a presentation ready for my course.

The event is on 12 November in Heathrow. I would be the first speaker of the event. Talk about baptism by fire!

9 November 2011

Today I sent off the first email to the Rent2Rent (R2R) mailing list. This is to invite people to look at our website and watch our YouTube video. I will be sending out the second email and releasing the second video on Friday.

The first email goes like this:

Massive Passive Income Secret Revealed

Hi Guys,

We hope that you are well.

This is Taiwo and Geoff here. We are corporate letting specialists. We met you at a recent property meeting/wealth propulsion seminar and we just want to tell you about a fantastic and unique strategy that we have been using to generate a huge passive income from property even when we do not own the property ourselves.

You can use this strategy to build a pension fund for yourself.

You can use this strategy to save up for a house.

You can use this strategy to build a pot of cash.

This is *truly* the ultimate an outlay of less than £4,000, which is all paid back to you within two weeks of starting.

Guys, we are releasing three videos over the next few days to explain to you exactly how we do it.

Our first video can now be viewed on our YouTube channel. Simply click on our website and click the YouTube button. In the meantime, you may like to have a look at our web site <www.renttorent.co.uk> to read our story and to learn more about us.

If you want to contact us in the meantime, please give a call or drop us an email. Our contact details are on our web site <www.renttorent.co.uk>.

We look forward to hearing from you.

Best regards,

Taiwo and Geoff

The Multi-Let Duo

P.S. Please remember to look into your email box in two days' time to view our second video.

Being focused

The purpose of this book is not to tell you how easy it has been for me to get to where I am today. It has been rather smooth, though, with a lot of ups and a few down moments. These down moments could have been significant if I had not focused on the results. I have to take a few pages just to cover this topic: Focus. My daily account is to show you that I never allowed myself the space to diverge from my focal point. I have had students who have given up before they even started. Others gave up after they had already done the hard work. This strategy is as easy to do as it is not to do.

I was reading Christopher Howard's book *Turning Passion into Profit*, the other day. He says, "Your focus creates your reality". I had never thought of this statement until I read it in his book, then I looked back at my journey since I came into the property industry just a year ago. I have taught this strategy to nine different people, and three are successfully applying it. The others have done absolutely nothing despite the fact that they also want to reap the results. And I have spoken about it to dozens of people but as far as I know, none of them is doing anything either.

So why have I become very successful at this at such an early age? Well, it is my focus. I focused on the result and the result only. Obstacles would have to be much greater than the result to divert my attention. For the past twelve months, I have devoured religiously two books a month and listened to personal development tapes. I stopped reading, listening to, and watching the news because there is no good news in the news. I have cleaned my system to prepare my mind and, most importantly, to focus my mind on the target. One cannot experience that on which they do not focus their attention.

I have been taught many strategies in the property business, none of them spoke to me personally. Some strategies are just a rip-off. I knew from day one where I wanted to see myself twelve months down the line. I knew how I would feel living that lifestyle. I knew what I would be wearing, where I would be having my lunches, in whose company I would be. I felt and lived the emotions of the results before I even found the way to get there.

By religiously focusing my attention on the result, somehow, the universe provided the missing elements for me to achieve it. Now, I am not trying to bathe anyone in religious beliefs here; what I am saying is that a strong focus on the result will carry you over any obstacle you might encounter on your way to where you wish to be.

It is very true: Our focus creates our reality.

That said, I have to get to Argos to get a Hoover and a kettle for one of the houses. I have to sort out the heater in one room and get some new beds delivered at my new house. Also I have to book my hotel room for 12 November, read some pages of the book I am reading at the moment, and finally, keep a couple of hours to do my Twitter assignment. Yes, I am now exploring other fields of passive income. I will tell you more in my next book. Yes, I am writing a second one.

11 November 2011

Today, I made my last attempt to get my money back from Bob, the Duo dude. Below is my wish to donate the sum to my charity of choice.

> Dear Bob, Tiffany,
>
> I hope you are all well. As per my last email to Tiffany, the £497 paid towards the speaker course is neither yours nor mine to keep. Unfortunately, our relationship has broken down due to the difference of opinions of what happened at the VIP meeting. I shall not go back into details.
>
> As I said, this £497 is not yours to keep. Please donate this money to the charity I have been supporting for many years. This will feed 300 children for a week or so. The link to the website is <http://www.homchildrenshome.org>; click on "How to help" to access their donation page.

A kind gesture of an additional 10 per cent would be honourable.

All the best,

Taiwo

12 November 2011

The Glenn Armstrong's niche cash flow event went well today. Geoff and I made a very good presentation—no nerves whatsoever.

This is the beginning of a bigger collaboration.

13 November 2011

Tenants from three houses contacted me claiming that some of their properties were missing. BOS71 had a blender and a hair clipper missing. GLO579 had pots and pans missing. They were all accusing Stacy, the cleaner. I had been having other complaints about this particular cleaner and she had been fired two days earlier. I called Stacy, left a message, then texted her. She texted me back asking me to call her back. I did, she did not acknowledge the accusations, but she immediately offered to pay for the items as long as I did not contact the police, a weird offer from a supposedly innocent person. I will have a meeting with her tomorrow at 4 p.m. to solve the problem.

14 November 2011

The case of the stolen shampoo, pans, and cooking oil continues.

More updates from Stacy: the items stolen have now extended to cooking oil, beans, and shampoo. She has agreed to refund all the items by the end of the week.

Today I had a meeting with two property investors who are also based in my area. They are starting a property club and they wanted me to be part of it. I have agreed to be included but in the HMO section alone, it being the topic I can talk about with ease.

If any of my readers have read *The Secret* by Rhonda Byrnes, you will know about the law of attraction. I have noticed that since I have focused my mind on the million, I have been meeting a lot more millionaires. It is just like when someone wants to buy a specific new car, he starts to see other people driving this car everywhere. This particular car did not just appear suddenly; it has been there and driven all along, but the new buyer never noticed it because it was not part of the information retained by his brain. This is exactly how I feel today; all my new friends are millionaires. The Glenn Armstrong event on Saturday probably put a dozen property millionaires in the same room and I was there to give them a speech.

My last room at CHU73 was rented today. It took us exactly eight days to rent out the house. Things have slowed down a bit as Christmas is approaching. Many people are returning to their countries. January will be a month to look forward to.

One of my agents called me last night to inform me of two new houses in my goldmine areas, one is for £1,100 and the other £895 pcm. I am seeing them tomorrow and will perhaps put an offer on them. That will give me a total number of sixteen houses. I intend to stop at twenty to take a break.

15 November 2011

I saw the two properties today. The Filton house for £895 is at a perfect location for Airbus and Rolls Royce employees. This should be fully tenanted within 2 weeks due to this being the slow period of the year. Mid November through the end December are slow months. The other house is also in my perfect area, just opposite where I already have a six-bedroom house and just few minutes away from most of my other properties. The house is big enough for five people. I made the mistake of not negotiating enough, which will now cost me £200 per month for 16 months. I did not think it through before accepting the house. I only pay £900 on average for all my houses in that area.

That aside, Rent2Rent (R2R) courses are now being booked: two more people have booked and three more asked for more information. I composed a standard email and below is a copy:

Hi,

We have had many requests regarding our course of 3 December 2011. This will be held at our office in Bristol. We will keep the special rate for this last course of the year. Below is all the information you need.

Location: Victoria Street, Bristol, BS1

Time: 9 a.m.-5.30 p.m.

Train Station: Temple Meads (a 15-minute walk)

Accommodation: Holiday Inn and Premier Inn

Links:

<www.holidayinn.com/hotels/us/en/bristol/brscc/hoteldetail>

<www.premierinn.com/en/hotel/BRIPLI/bristol-city-centre-king-street>

Meals: Lunch, teas, coffees, and snacks will be provided on the day, free of charge. (You will need that!)

What to bring: Your laptop and your local paper

Special one off rate: £497 VAT included.

Available seats: 10 only (we cannot take more than this number due to the live demos) first come first served.

If you have any further queries, please email me and I will reply as soon as I get it.

We are looking forward to your success!

Taiwo and Geoff

The Multi-Let Duo

The webinar is also in full swing. Our first one is for thirty minutes and will happen in just a few days. We left it until the last moment because we only have limited seats at our training days; we can afford that luxury. The webinar email goes like this:

Hi Guys,

Geoff and I will be presenting a thirty-minute webinar on Thursday evening, 17 November 2011, at 8 p.m. We will share with you all about our tried and tested "Niche Cash Flow Strategy" for making returns on investment (ROI) of up to 100 per cent per annum, by renting out individual rooms to corporate working tenants from properties that we do not even own *for an initial outlay/investment of less than £4,000!*

Guys, if you are *really serious about making money* and you really want to make a *Massive Passive Income* out of properties that *you do not even own,* listen to us and ask us questions this Thursday evening at 8 p.m.

Title: Niche Cash Flow Strategy—"How to Generate up to 100 Per Cent Return On Investment by Corporate Letting"

Date: Thursday, 17 November 2011

Time: 8 p.m.-9 p.m. GMT

After registering, you will receive a confirmation email containing information about joining the Webinar.

Space is limited.

Reserve your webinar seat now at:

<www3.gotomeeting.com/register/977292630>

See you soon!

Taiwo and Geoff

18 November 2011

The webinar went very well without any interference. I cannot believe that we are now up and running. Imagine where we will be in six months' time.

I composed an email to thank all the attendees and those who could not make it. The webinar was recorded and a link provided for everyone to catch up. The email is as follows:

> Hi Guys,
>
> Geoff and I had a wonderful time last night doing our very first webinar. We wish to thank those who attended. We had so many questions we couldn't answer them all on the call. Feel free to send us an email and we will try to answer as quickly as possible.
>
> For those who could not attend, we have recorded the whole webinar and you can download it by just clicking on the link below. Please follow the instructions so that you are not bombarded with advertising.
>
> We look forward to your success!
>
> Taiwo and Geoff

<www.sendspace.com/file/0c2qb2>

(Please note for the download above: This is a "free", large, file download site, so you might get bombarded with advertising links on the pages. Sometimes these will take you to another page before you are able to download the recordings. If this happens, ignore the big blue link that says, "Download" on the first page, and instead click on the blue box underneath that says "Regular Download". This will take you to another page where, again, ignore all the advertising links and the big green "Download" and "Play Now" buttons. You *must* click on the light blue box in the middle of the screen that says, "Click here to start download from sendspace".)

Some questions that people asked during the webinar are below:

FAQs

JULIE asks, "I live in West London. Can this strategy be used in any town/city in the UK?"

Answer: Yes, of course it can.

Alan asks, "What is the ideal number of tenants to have in one of your multi-letting properties?

Answer: Minimum four, but five or more give fantastic *profits!*

Susanne asks, "I live in Leeds. I do not have tens of thousands of pounds to put down as deposit money to buy a house. So as a new person looking to get into property, what are the best areas in which to do multi-letting?"

Answer: Leeds is a fantastic city to do corporate letting. You have the second-largest financial centre outside of London right at your doorstep! Lots of corporate professionals are looking for accommodation. St James's

Hospital (St Jimmy's) is the largest hospital in the UK, employing more than 8,000 staff (hospital staff are wonderful tenants to house!). There is also the huge red brick University of Leeds, full of students looking for accommodation. Leeds also has a railway station and a motorway system!

Susanne, believe me, Leeds has everything going for it as regards to multi-letting to corporate employees or to whomever you want to rent a house!

Cynthia asks, "Please explain again to me, how soon after the tenants take the room do you get your initial investment money back?"

ANSWER: The day that the renter takes possession of the room, he/she gives you one months' rent in advance and one months' rent as a deposit!

Stephen asks, "Please clarify how to find private owners and landlords of properties for multi-letting?"

ANSWER: Websites advertising rooms/houses to let, newspaper advertisements in local property papers, estate agents and letting agents.

Do you tell letting agents that you are going to sublet?

ANSWER: We do not use the word "sublet"; we tell them that we are going to put corporate tenants in the houses. As long as the letting agent does corporate let, then there should be no problem at all.

Setting Goals

I will close this book with the subject of goals setting. It is important to know where one is heading in this game. This is such a cash-rich strategy and one might be compelled to spend a lot without even noticing. I would advise you, reader, to set up a three-month goal chart, which will enable you to move quickly and efficiently on your journey. How much do you want to earn in passive income in the next three months? Be realistic. This figure must be what you have achieved on your first property plus or minus 10 per cent. Make sure you review this goal every day just to keep yourself on track.

It is often said that we always overestimate our yearly goals and underestimate our lifetime goals. I set myself a one-year goal and I hit that within eight months. There is no reason you should not hit yours in half that time.

As we approach the end of November 2011, I am ahead of the goals I set myself in January 2011. I have now reached my target £10K a month in passive income. I am now about to sign three other contracts with three new landlords. This means additional twenty rooms to be added to my portfolio. Here ends the journey in this first book, the story to be continued in volume 2 of the journey.

REFERENCES

Useful books

It is important to keep the desire burning even when times are hard. These are some of the books that worked for me in terms of building my mental strength.

Bach, David, *Smart Women Finish Rich.*

Byrne, Rhonda, *The Secret.*

Canfield, Jack and Mark Victor Hansen, *Chicken Soup for the Soul.*

Carnegie, Dale, *How to Develop Self-confidence and Influence People by Public Speaking.*

Carnegie, Dale, *How to Win Friends and Influence People.*

Conti, Peter and David Finkel, *Multiple Streams Of Income.*

Dennis, Felix, *How to Get Rich.*

Endlich, Lisa, *Goldman Sachs.*

Fielding, Gill, *The Book of Riches.*

Frankl, Viktor E., *Man's Search for Meaning.*

Gladwell, Malcolm, *The Outliers.*

Gladwell, Malcolm, *The Tipping Point.*

Godin, Seth, *Purple Cow*.

Godin, Seth, *Tribes*.

Goldstein, Noah J., Steve J. Martin and Robert Cialdini, *Yes!*

Howard, Christopher, *Turning Passion into Profits*.

Jeffers, Susan, *Feel the Fear and Do It Anyway*.

Julien, Steve, *House Share Hero*.

Kiyosaki, Robert T., *Rich Dad Poor Dad*.

Kiyosaki, Robert T., *Rich Dad's Retire Young Retire Rich*.

Kiyosaki, Robert T., *Unfair Advantage*.

Olson, Jeff, *The Slight Edge*.

Proctor, Bob, *You Were Born Rich*.

Ribbon, Paul, *Hustle Your Way to Property Success*.

Stanley, Thomas J. and William D. Danko, *The Millionaire Next Door*.

Walsch, Neale Donald, *Conversation with God*.

Useful websites:

Your local city council website should be your first point of contact when using Rent2Rent strategy.

<www.renttorent.co.uk>

<www.landlordzone.co.uk>

<www.legalcentre.co.uk>

<www.rightmove.co.uk>

<www.gumtree.co.uk>

<www.easyroommate.co.uk>

<www.spareroom.co.uk>

Useful helpful courses, which might help provide further knowledge in the property industry

<www.renttorent.co.uk>

<www.glennarmstrong.com>

<www.hmodaddy.co.uk>

Useful networking events that might help you meet other like-minded investors

TENANTS: THE GOOD, THE BAD, AND THE DOWNRIGHT UGLY

Tenants in this sample have been assigned aliases as I do not want the guilty to feel embarrassed, at least not too much.

I remember my handyman, Graham, asking me one day, "When does one know when a tenant is lying?" The response was: "The moment he opens his mouth."

After a year of managing tenants, the truth cannot be clearer. There is a huge difference between tenants born and bred in the UK and tenants born and bred outside the UK. I have come to recognise that part of the population that will cause me grief. I have learned to avoid them. It is not discrimination, it is business. Can you pay the rent? If the answer is yes, you can stay. If not, then keep walking, my dear!

My first funny story came from one of my earlier tenants; we will call him Manu. Manu arrived at one of my houses after been kicked out by his previous housemates. He told me some stories, which I then believed to be true—naively, of course., On one occasion, Manu texted me at midnight to complain about some noise in his room. I got the text later in the morning. Then he called me that very morning to complain again about these strange noises. Coming from an African background, I started thinking about ghost stories, etc. Then I asked Manu to describe the noise; he uttered a sound that sounded a bit like the wind. Then I asked him to open his window to listen if he could still hear the sound? Yes, he could. He was afraid of the whistling of the wind!

My second story is a man who I will name Lee. Lee took one of my newest rooms. I had by then been in this game for twelve months and I had seen time and time again the kind of lies most tenants tell. Lee took a room in a four-bedroom, newly renovated house. After three weeks in the house, Lee contacted my assistant to say that one of the windows in the sitting room had just been smashed and needed to be fixed. I was then away on a business trip. My assistant called me to ask me what to do. I told him to ask for the person who had opened the window, because for this type of window to break, the person who had opened it must have lifted it too high towards the ceiling and then released it suddenly. So this person would have to pay for the repairs. The message was passed on to the tenants, and then I told them I would pop over the following day to see the damage done.

When I arrived at the house, Lee was angry and surprised that he would have to pay for his action. He immediately confronted me with, "I think you have bigger problems to solve in the house because my room is full of mould". I simply responded, "If you have mould in your room, it is because you do not ventilate it enough. Again, that is your responsibility." Surprised and amazed by my lack of compassion, he immediately brought up his connection with someone in the council, as all guilty tenants do according to my experience. I told him to bring his contact in to have a look. I gave him a printout about how to deal with mould, with anti-mould solutions for him to use. He expected me to do the cleaning for him. I told him to put his gloves on and start scrubbing. He was amazed at my request; he then decided to be the tenant from hell.

Tenants want everything but want to pay for nothing. Tenants want somebody to carry their responsibilities for them. How can you, as a landlord, deal with their expectations? How can you, as a landlord, take control of whatever may come and throw it back at them? How can you, as a landlord, re-educate them to understand that you are not Tony Blair or their parent?

I personally believe that Tony Blair's policies have crippled a whole generation of people in this country. He has taken away from many, the duty to be self reliant. Instead, most people born and bred in the UK believe that after leaving mum and dad, it is the landlord's turn to carry them further along in life. Then it is the turn of the state or their employers. The lack of responsibility for one's actions is apparent, which is why many landlords fail and give up.

Back to Lee, he became the worst tenant I have had up to this stage. The full story will be continued in the next book. You really will not want to miss this one!